Acknowledgements

This book is the result of the active collaboration of hundreds of participants in my Master's classes and professional development workshops. I am deeply appreciative of everyone's stories, insights, objections, ah-ha moments, suggestions, comments, post class emails, phone calls and beer conversations. All have been helpful.

There are, however a few people who deserve special mention for their on-going dialogue with this long project. Dan Ebener, Ron Wastyn, Rick Dienesch, Dave O'Connell, Patrick O'Leary and Fred Smith – who could ask for more generous, intelligent and caring colleagues.

Among workshop participants another few also standout, Steve Ambrosi, Kent Pilcher, Susan Zelnio, Terry Predmore, George Hollins, Jennifer Van Dyke, Eric White – all come to mind as being regularly a part of this conversation.

Finally, I must recognize my late friend Wayne Slabon who recognized early on that we were doing something special in our classes and workshops. Every time I teach a class or step into a workshop, I am aware of Wayne's presence and contributions to my work. He gone but he has not left me.

Randy

Table of Contents

Introduction

Managing workplace conflicts remains a stubborn and ubiquitous problem for most organizations. We have been teaching university master classes, conducting professional workshops and coaching individuals on conflict since 2004. The vast majority of the people we interact with are supervisors and mid management folks with a sprinkling of executives. The work place conflicts that swirl around them plague, confuse and frustrate them and their conflict dance partners. We call them "dance partners" because we see the give and take of the conversation over our conflicts as a kind of dance. The normal tendency is to see these conflicts as contests of wills, struggles to get those with whom we have the conflict to accept our point of view. In these cases, we are more likely to see those with whom we have a conflict as a kind of opponent. If instead we reconceive of these conflicts differently, then we have a better chance of approaching our handling of them in a more effective manner. To see this as a kind of dance where both parties need each other in order to accomplish what is important to each of them is a more promising approach. We view this as the beginning of a more fundamental mindset shift.

This book is for and about their workplace conflicts. We have aimed at one on one disputes

- disputes between co-workers
- between bosses and subordinates,
- between customers and frontline employees,
- between suppliers and purchasers,

- between subcontractors and contract managers

These folks are working in good faith, trying as best they can to 'make things work'. When our dance partners are reasonable and committed, then we can normally muddle our way through to at least a compromise solution.

But often conflicts get the better of us. Mostly our approaches are hit or miss, guided by a kind of natural, instinctual quid pro quo approach. If our dance partners appear to us as hard positional bargainers, who seek resolution through intimidation or domination or simply don't respond to resolution overtures, we give what we get. We push back with the same hard positional approach. We become more stubborn and dominant ourselves. Sometimes this works. More often it does not.

What is lacking is training in how to manage conflict. More specifically, how to manage it in a particular way. We have written this book to approach conflict in a very particular way – we call it the 'search for the integrative space.' We did not make this approach up, although we believe the particular phrase is unique to us. Others have been aware and supportive of the practice of integrative conflict management. As far back as 1925, the brilliant, not now largely forgotten, Mary Parker Follett wrote: "There are three main ways of dealing with conflict: domination, compromise and integration." Domination is what we would call the win-lose approach, the tour de force victory of one party over the other. Compromises, she identifies, as the most common way that most people try to deal with conflict. Each sides "gives up a little" in order to reach an agreement. The third way, integration, differs significantly.

Integration . . . "involves invention, and the clever thing to do is to recognize this, and not to let one's think stay within the boundaries of two alternatives which are mutually exclusive."

Parker Follett goes on to point out integration is seldom even considered. What was true in 1925, remains just as valid today. She also points out that we lack the training to find integrative solutions to overcome our tendency is always "beat the other side." She observes that employers typically try "to force through" their previous conceived ideas rather than engage in a genuine exchange of ideas.

Now neither Parker Follett nor I are so naïve to think that there is always an integrative solution for all of our conflicts or that integrative problem solving is a magic bullet that **assassinates** our organizational villains. Rather we are asserting that the search for an integrative solution represents a superior approach to both command and compromise as a conflict management method. We believe that the opportunity to find an integrative solution presents itself much more often than most of us are aware. If we all became more aware of those possibilities and we became more skillful at practicing it, then this would bring enormous benefits to our organizations and communities. This then it what this book seeks to call attention to.

*****

Thinking about the success of integrative conflict management calls to our mind an analogy with MLB batting averages.

Question: What is the difference between a .250 hitter and a .333 hitter? Answer: The Hall of Fame and several million dollars a year.

Question: What is the difference *in performance at the plate* between a .250 hitter and a .333 hitter?
Answer: The .250 hitter gets 3 hits in 12 at bats. The .333 hitter gets 4 hits in 12 at bats. That's it! *Just 1 more hit in 12 at bats.*

Question: How hard is it to get just one more hit in 12 at bats?
Answer: Turns out, pretty damn hard.

According to the ESPN MLB Batting Stats for 2016, in the American League only Jose Altuve of the Astro's hit more than .333 at .338. Out of the 75 players listed only he hit .333 plus or 1.3%. In the National League, two players DJ LeMahieu at .348 and Daniel Murphy at .347 out of 67 players listed hit .333 or over or 3%. MLB taken together is 3 out of 142 or 2.1%. http://www.espn.com/mlb/stats/batting

Why is this so hard? The batter must judge the speed and exact location of the pitch without knowing either how fast or where exactly the ball will be when it crosses the plate. A batter has .395 seconds to hit a ball (diameter = 2.9") travelling at 95 mph with a bat (diameter = 3" to 4"). Despite the endless repetitions of the mantra "keep your eye on the ball" by tens of thousands of coaching devotees, it turns out that is not possible to do the whole way. Of course, the pitcher does everything he can to make this more difficult. Toss in a bit of luck or lack thereof and viola, 2% success rate.

Continuing with the batting average metaphor, no one bats 1.000 in resolving conflicts. No matter how good we are, we are not going to find a successful integrative solution to all of our conflicts. Why is this so hard?

First, our instincts and natural intuitions work against us. These evolved on the savannahs of Africa over 4 million years ago to help us eat and keep from being eaten. What evolved as critical then often gets in our way now as we try to work out complicated social relationships. These "built-ins", as we will see later in the book, lead us astray as we try to manage our conflicts.

Second, this means that we have to learn how to manage conflict. Aristotle writes, "Excellence is an art won by training and habituation." Like any finely honed skill, i.e. hitting a baseball, we need practice under expert guidance to achieve excellence. We have plenty of opportunities to practice managing conflicts; we live in a "practice rich environment". What we lack most often is expert guidance. We find very few schools at any level teaching integrative conflict management. Learning on the job is often under the instruction of people who themselves don't know how to do it well. For whom, commanding and compromise appear to be their only choices.

We can read books and articles that provide some instruction on the matter; however the quality of that advice varies widely from expert to just guessing. Additionally, there are few sustained treatments and examination of integrative conflict management. Even when the written advice is expert and solid, we have to recognize and recall how to apply it. Until the expert guidance replaces our in-born instinctual responses, success depends on recollection – an uncertain and uneven mechanism.

Third, many of our conflicts are a surprise to us. Like an inside fastball, conflicts comes on us with a speed and in a location, we didn't expect.

By the time we realize what is happening, it is often too late to get a successful integrative "hit". If we could improve our conflict anticipation skills, that would be a big help.

How can this book help us?

Conflict and Collaboration will help people who work in a variety of organizations get an extra integrative "hit" or two in the next few conflict at bats. We are confident that we can get the reader those extra hits that they are missing today. Ted Williams, the greatest hitter of all-time, hit .344 lifetime in 19 years – a remarkable achievement. But it means that even "Teddy Ballgame" was unsuccessful more than 6 times out of 10. No one bats 1.000, so lesson one is *relax*.

Some conflicts for whatever reason, we will never resolve or even manage well. We can concentrate on the ones we can and stop chasing the bad "pitches". We can increase our integrative average. We don't pretend to have "the answer" to every conflict.

Conflict and Collaboration attempts to synthesize and incorporate the research from several sources to emphasize a conflict management approach we call *the search for the integrative space*. We draw heavily from experts like Mary Parker Follett, Kenneth Thomas, Roger Fisher, William Ury, Edgar Schein, David Bohm, William Isaac, Freidrich Glasl, Thomas Jordan, Daniel Kahneman, Otto Scharmer, Daniel Simon, and Michael Marquardt among others.

Conflict and Collaboration more than any other book on conflict management stresses the *centrality of perspective* in the conflict process in all its phases from awareness to possible resolution. Other writings recognize that perspective plays *a role*. Here we insist it plays *the role* in conflict. This recognition of the centrality of each parties' perspective, much of which is unconscious and intuitive, requires a serious re-orientation to our conflict partners' interactions. The reader begins to appreciate the importance of loosening their certainty of having a privileged position in understanding and trying to address both parties' conflict concerns.

Conflict and Collaboration focuses exclusively on adopting collaborative approaches and techniques in an effort to arrive at solutions that integrate the perspectives of both conflict partners. Its sole purpose seeks to stimulate the reader to look primarily for solutions that incorporates the concerns and perspectives of both conflict partners. We recognize, of course, that it is not always possible to find the integrative solution space. However, our experience has been that the vast majority of people never even conceive of an integrative solution. Or if they can conceive of it theoretically, they fail to recognize it in practice. We are taught from infancy onward that compromise is the best approach to conflict. We disagree. The search for the integrative space is a better approach. A book exclusively dedicated to this approach would help address this deficiency. Plenty of other places for readers to go if they want to improve the ability to get more from compromises.

Conflict and Collaboration demonstrates that increased understanding of the conflict issues and improved interpersonal relationship with our dance partners are critical for successful conflict management. Each step in our method measures itself against that dual standard. We must keep asking,

"Will this action increase our understanding of the conflict issue? What will be the effect of this action on our relationship seen from the perspective of the other person?"

Conflict and Collaboration, therefore, advocates dialogue rather than debate, discussion or arguing. True conversation becomes the preferred method of interpersonal communication during conflict episodes. Dialogue produces the highest possibility of increasing and making explicit our perspectives on the conflict issue in a manner rooted in respect and concern for the other party.

Conflict and Collaboration makes explicit the tendency of pursuing distributive solutions (compromises) to escalate conflicts. This makes even the compromise solutions we are seeking more difficult to achieve. Thus, even when the search for the integrative space does not result in integrative solution, the methodology of dialogue improves the clarity of the conflict issue and maintains or improves the relationship of the conflict partners. Both lead to an increased likelihood of Fisher and Ury called "principled compromise".

Conflict and Collaboration introduces the heuristic device of "the neutral statement of the conflict" as a technique to bring clarity and specificity to the conflict sources from both parties' perspectives in a way that improves the relationship. The neutral statement of the conflict creates the separation of the person from the problem that is critical to integrative solutions. It also creates the preconditions for diagnosing the sources of the conflict.

Conflict and Collaboration delineates and makes explicitly clear the three sources or types of conflicts: factual conflicts, interest conflicts and behavioral expectation conflicts. Learning to recognize which source generates the conflict is a critical diagnostic activity that needs to precede resolution attempts. Most advice on managing conflicts overlooks the importance of identifying these three sources of conflict. It plays a central role in our integrative methodology.

Conflict and Collaboration creates a "solution path" for each of these types of conflict. The solution paths describe particular activities that need to take place to increase the chances of successful integration of perspectives. The solution path for factual conflicts differs from the solution path for interest conflicts. These differ still from the solution path for behavioral expectation conflicts. This approach creates an advantage for everyday practitioners because it gives them some rails to run on rather than just trying to guess what to do next. It is no guarantor of success but it increases our chances.

How the book is laid out

The sections of the book generally follow the "Conflict Episode" figure laid out by Kenneth Thomas in his article "Conflict and Negotiation Process in Organizations", Chapter 11 in *Handbook of Industrial and Organizational Psychology*, Vol. 3, 2nd ed., (pp. 651-717). We have been using the conflict episode as the central focal point in our classes and workshops. It has proven to be effective in getting people to grasp the dynamics of the conflict process and apply it to their everyday workplace struggles. Thomas's meta-review provided a comprehensive over view of all of the conflict literature up to that point. Thomas wrote it for an academic audience. We, on the other hand, are trying to help folks in their everyday work place conflicts. Some of what Thomas covers in less detail, like the sources of conflict, we have expanded into more significance for the everyday employee. Other material, for example, on compromising or structural conditions, etc., we have left out because that is not the focus of our approach. Beyond that, based on our long years of experience in getting people to understand and apply Thomas's and other's concepts, *Conflict and Collaboration* provides more examples and approaches that resonate with people in the work place.

At the end of every section, the reader will find "Restorying Exercises". All of our classes and workshops use the restorying technique for conflict management. We have added these exercises at the end of each chapter to replicate the learning experience for the reader. Unfortunately, we cannot provide the conversational exchanges and interpersonal interactions that a class or workshop can. Nonetheless, even the written restorying provides value. Perhaps our readers can find a partner with whom they can share their conflict stories as they go through the book.

Restorying is a teaching method based on social constructivism; that is, we learn best within the context of the problem we are trying to understand. Restorying employs successive repetitions of writing and rewriting and discussing personal, learner-generated conflict stories to promote conceptual application, critical thinking, and problem solving skills in conflict situations for which there is no obvious solution.

The restorying approach emphasizes learning about integrative conflict management through personal story application and story sharing. The restorying approach offers a potentially viable alternative because the author was dissatisfied with conventional case studies. Conventional case studies often fall short in providing the desired range or complexity of problem space elements. On the other hand, it may embed problems in contexts that are not learner relevant. They are too neat, too canned and designed more for the professor to show off because they had "the answer" to the problem. In real life, in these kind of situations, "the answer" is a fiction. Moreover, the sustained analysis of a past personal experience may result in deeper internalization of subject content and transfer of learning. Traditional case studies are devoid of any emotional connection to the learner. Lack of emotion diminishes the motivation to learn.

While restorying may not be appropriate for some learning contexts, it holds promise for settings that can incorporate the key elements and address the adoption considerations described in this book. The restorying approach invites the reader to consider how their personal, conflict relevant stories may be employed, shared, reflected upon, revised, expanded upon, and redeployed to promote achievement of desired learning outcomes. For a fuller explanation of this methodology, see the article:

"Learning by Restorying", Slabon, Wayne A.; Richards, Randy L.; Dennen, Vanessa P.

Instructional Science: An International Journal of the Learning Sciences, v42 n4 p505-521 Jul 2014

Definition

Following Ken Thomas, we start with defining conflict as

. . . the process that begins when one party perceives that the other party has negatively affected or is about to negatively affect, something that he or she cares about. ("Conflict and Negotiation Process in Organizations")

Thomas notes that this definition is simple, implies interdependence and interaction, and is broad enough to cover a wide variety of types of concerns.

Unpacking this definition, first, we notice that both parties do not have to be aware that there is a conflict. The party whose concerns are negatively affected may choose not to act on those concerns. If so, then the party whose actions created the conflict remains unaware that they have done so. They may never know or they may find out much later that they had inadvertently created a conflict. Not long ago, we found out that something we said and was misrepresented created a conflict for someone eight years ago. They never brought it to our attention and have been harboring ill will and hurt feelings over it for eight years.

Second, consider all the things that we care about in life. If we made a list of all the things we cared about, how long would that list be? Twenty items? Fifty? A hundred? More? In any case, it would be a long list. Now think about how many people we interact with every day. How many is that? Ten? Twenty? More? What are the chances that during the day one of those people will say or do something that negatively affects what we care about? You're right – a very high chance. Now consider this in the other direction. What are that chances that we, simply by going about our daily tasks, will negatively affect one of the dozens of concerns from the dozens of people with whom we interact? Right, higher.

We cannot live among each other without generating conflict ourselves or having others around us generate conflict for us. Once we understand conflict is about threatening each other concerns, we can see there is no way to avoid it.

> **Conflict is the sea we must learn to swim in.**

At the beginning of our workshops, some participants say, "I don't have any conflicts." Once they understand this definition, they realize they have multiple conflicts. Or, people will say, "I avoid conflicts". We now see that there is no way to avoid conflicts. What these people mean is that they choose not to respond to the conflicts that they have; they chose not to respond to the actions that negatively affect their concerns.

This highlights a common confusion of mistaking our response to the conflict as the conflict itself. The Sixth Patriarch of Chan (Chinese Zen) around 650 expressed the koan that "The finger pointing at the moon is not the moon."

Similarly, the response to the conflict is not the conflict – rather it points to the conflict. Avoiding

> The response to the conflict points to the conflict.
>
> It is not the conflict.

responding to the conflict is one of the two most common ways of dealing with conflict. The other is to argue. People often confuse the argument for the conflict itself as if the argument was the conflict, "I had a really bad conflict today. We ended up shouting at each other." They chose to respond to the threat to what they cared about by arguing but the conflict itself was over their threatened concerns. The argument points to the conflict but it is not the conflict.

Third, the definition helps us see that either of us can generate the conflict. In our workshops and classes, the conflict stories that people tell almost always relate that their dance partner has initiated the conflict. Once, we unravel the stories, however, it becomes apparent that many of them had actually done something that negatively affected what their dance partner cared about. The others were simply responding in kind. This most often comes as something of a shock largely because of our inability to look at the conflict from the other person's perspective.

Four, the definition as to who initiates the conflict carries with it no moral weight. Just because one party did something that negatively affected what someone else cares about does not mean that they did something "wrong". All organizational change efforts generate conflict. The change effort will negatively affect anyone who benefits from the status quo. We point out to project managers that it is a necessary part of their job to generate conflict. As we noted before, even just going about our daily activities may negatively affect others' concerns. Most often, this is inadvertent because we have focused on our tasks and the effect on others is unknown to us.

The conflict process begins with this awareness of the threat to what we care about. The rest of the process has a predictable structure and dynamic – it moves in a way we can anticipate. We can think of this process unfolding like the scenes of a play. If we can understand the conflict dynamic, we can identify those points in the drama most likely to result in outcomes that are more positive. We will examine this process in detail later in the book. But next, we want to explore the central role that perspectives play in all our conflicts. Before we get to that chapter, let's complete Exercise 1 below.

Exercise 1: Restorying your conflict: The beginning

We learn best from listening to stories and telling our own stories. Creating your own conflict story is a powerful way to get the full impact of the material from the book. You should write your story out. As we move through the material, you will have a number of opportunities to re-tell your story (restorying) that will let you look at your story in a new framework. This restorying is a highly effective way of helping you understand and apply the lessons from the book. Once you learn to do it with your own story, you will be better prepared to do it with your future stories and with the conflict stories you see around you.

Think of a conflict that you and one other person have had on the job. You want to choose one that had more than has some legs – goes beyond one incident. You want to choose one where both parties knew there was a conflict. Here is the outline form to get you started. We will be expanding on this as we move forward.

1. Name of your conflict dance partner. If this is for your eyes only, you can use their real name. If you are thinking about sharing this with others, I suggest an alias.

2. Their relationship to you – boss, subordinate, co-worker, customer, supplier, etc…

3. What is it that they said or did that negatively affected what you cared about? (Or if you originated the conflict, what did you say or do?) Try to be as specific as possible.

4. How did what they said or did negatively affect what you cared about? Again, being as specific as possible makes a big difference. This helps us think more deeply about what we (or they) care about. Knowing what each party cares about is central

to our approach. So it is never too early to probing the concerns of all parties.

5. What was your immediate response to this?

Write this out in the form a brief story. Tell it only about the original incident. Don't cover the whole story. You will be expanding on this as we go.

You will find these exercises even more effective if you can find a partner or two or three or more with whom you can share this exploration of the conflict and collaboration. I suggest using the book as a guide for you and your partners' reflection on your own conflict experiences.

Changing the way you envision conflict and integrative solutions will open up new possibilities that have previously escaped your notice.

Dialoging with your partners is a superior way to create this new mind set.

Centrality of perspectives

Our approach to conflict management begins with an examination of the centrality of perspective in the conflict process. The perspectives of each of the conflict dance partners determines nearly everything about the conflict: what is or is not a conflict, the parties' emotional responses, their initial actions in response to the threat to what they care about, their willingness to cooperate, and whether they will choose the distributive or integrative strategies and tactics.

Most popular material on conflict management make *some* reference to the issue of perspective usually a kind of off-handed recognition about trying to understand the other party's point of view. One of the best treatments of perspectives in conflict and negotiations is found in Roger Fisher's and Scott Brown's book, *Getting Together: Building Relationships While We Negotiate*. Fisher and Brown make frequent reference to and suggestions about understanding the issues from the other person's perspective. We highly recommend that book.

In contrast, many writings on conflict management do not even mention it. This discounting of the role of perspective becomes most obvious when we examine those writings regarding how they frame the reader's role in the conflict. Almost all assume (take the perspective) that we, as the reader, have the privileged point of view in the conflict. We have correctly analyzed the situation. We have the key insights. Our vision charts the course for a bright future. We know best how to implement the mission. Our dance partner, on the other hand, generally suffers from some form of personal dysfunction, social disorder or organizational myopia in those texts. These books and articles inform us that our job in handling the conflict is to get the other person to see the light – that is, to view the conflict from our perspective. This same blind spot appears for most treatments of organizational change which, given the fact that all organizational change generates conflict, should come as no surprise.

Essentially, the approach assumes our job is to *fix our dance partner* through various techniques and tools for persuasion. Understanding their perspective helps us select the right levers for moving them to see things correctly, i.e. the way we want the conflict resolved. Rarely, do these authors call into question our own perspective or the role it plays in generating the conflict. Few are the suggestions for re-examining how we have framed the conflict. God forbid, we should suspect that our own perspective is itself central to the conflict process. The suggestion that we might misunderstand the situation never enters into consideration.

These approaches to conflict management do not challenge the reader's perspective of their conflicts. As authors of our own conflict stories, we rarely question our perspectives in our conflicts.

In contrast, our approach in this book emphasizes the dominant role of perspective in our conflicts. This includes our perspective and the

> We are more inclined to see the conflict by pointing out the window than by peering in the mirror.

perspective of our conflict dance partners. In some cases, we may have examined and made explicit fragments of our perspective. More often and more importantly, large areas of our perceptions and perspectives remain hidden from our conscious awareness. We rarely take the time in conflict situations to scrutinize our own underlying assumptions, personal values, or interests. To make matters more complicated, we project our own fear and anxieties onto our dance partner's intentions, values and actions obscuring a more realistic understanding of their actions. Of course, the same applies to the way they act and react in the conflict situation towards us. Most likely, they have not made the difficult effort of self-examination of their own perceptions and perspectives of our conflict. Similarly, they project their fears and anxieties on to our intentions, values and actions.

Recognizing all of this liberates us from the constraints that our perspective places on us during our conflicts. No longer imprisoned by our perspective, we can now see possibilities that previously were hidden from us. We are no longer restricted to the view from the narrow confines of our experiential prison. We loosen our grip regarding our certitude and desire to be "right" in our conflicts. We can listen our way, in the phrase of Otto Scharmer, to create an "open mind, open heart and open will". These mindset changes are necessary for turning conflict into a search for the integrative space.

Let's break our conflict perspective down into three parts: 1) my perspective on the conflict situation 2) my perspective about myself 3) my perspective on my conflict dance partner.

My perspective on the situation:
1. What the conflict issue(s) is (are).
2. The conflict causes.
3. Who else might be involved or affected?
4. The conflict's history.
5. How it began.
6. Where is likely to go.

My perspective about myself:
1. How does this affect what I care about?
2. What my position on the issue is.
3. What I want the conflict outcome to be.
4. What I think might be the best way(s) to get what I want.
5. What my role in the conflict is.
6. How I have been behaving in the conflict?
7. My intentions – what should I do about this?

My perspective on my dance partner:
1. What they are asking of me.
2. What is their role in the conflict?

3. What is their position on the issue.

4. What they want the conflict outcome to be.

5. Their intentions – what they should do about this?

6. How they are behaving in the conflict.

Obviously, my conflict dance partner operates from their perspective on these three areas as well. Clearly, all of this complicates the matter of trying to envision an integrative solution, let alone trying to create one.

Roger Fisher and Scott Brown's book, *Getting Together: Building Relationships as We Negotiate*, does an admirable job of bringing to light the importance of differing perspectives. In Chapter 3, they point out that

If our disagreements are significant, we will almost certainly have strikingly dissimilar perceptions of ourselves, of each other, of what is important of what our relationship is today and of what it might become.

A number of factors color the perspectives of both of the conflict parties on these questions. Our perspectives are certainly shaped by our DNA, by how we were raised, by our occupational history, by our age, by our birth order, by our education, by our race, our ethnicity, by our gender, by our sexual orientation, by our economic class, by our social status, by our current family status, by our recreational choices, by our religion and by country in which we grew up and the region of the country in which we grew up. They will also be shaped by a particular existential personal experience especially situations of significant loss.

Beyond these factors, our memories of prior experiences with our conflict dance partner will shape our perspective in this current conflict. Our memories of the prior experiences rather than the prior experiences themselves are what we recall from our perspective. Following Daniel Kahneman, we are calling attention to the distinction between what we actually experience and what we remember from that experience. We recognize that our memories play an critical role in our perspective surrounding the conflict.

Why does this matter? Evidence abounds regarding the unreliability of our memories. Despite the fact that most people think their memories act like some kind of video camera, research makes it clear that our memories are to a large degree 'constructed'. Tzofit Ofengenden points out that neuroscientists now believe that memory, especially autobiographical memory, is not stable (has never been stable). Autobiographical memories are susceptible to multiple influences and are liable to distortions and deceptions. Hence, we cannot rely on them as fully accurate representations. At the same time, however, these memory changes occur without us being aware of them. Unfortunately, we still naively believe in our memories and view them as accurate representations of our past.

Current research in memories suggest that episodic autobiographical memories are in a constant state of adjustment depending on the demands of the reason for the recall. Each new memory retrieval alters the memory recalled. So current events connected to our past memories have a good chance of altering the past memory in the very process of recalling it. Hence, integrating new elements into an activated memory forms a new version of the original episodic memory.

If our memories are constructed and reconstructed as part of a dynamic process of which we are unaware, then how confident should we be of our belief about these past events relevant to our conflict situation? Ofengenden emphasizes that we unconsciously integrate apparent supporting evidences from the present into our memory to help us fit our recollection into consistency with the present.

In fact, this means that my recollection of my autobiographical episodes, the ones most critical in conflict situations, is not an examination of the original event but a constant process of comparing my current memory with my past memory of the original memory of the original event. Each recollection removing me one more memory event from the previous memory event until, if I am aware and honest about this, I can no longer assert with confidence that I remember what really happened.

Daniel Kahneman tells a story of his encounter with a German SS soldier as a Jewish child one night in the dark streets of Paris. The encounter had a profound effect on him in terms of the complexity and unexpected outcome. Kahneman in reflecting on this story realizes that he has told it so many times, he can no longer be sure of what exactly happened that night. He recognizes that with each retelling (and there have been dozens) there has been some alteration of the original memory. So today, even as he tells the story, he is not confident of all of its details.

My memories and those of my dance partner of our past interactive episodes will be different, perhaps even radically different. For both of us, these constructed and reconstructed memories define the quality and tenor of our current relationship relevant to the conflict. Do I like this person? Do I think the person likes me? How much can I trust them? How concerned are they about me? What kind of respect have they shown me? How have they treated me in the past? Were they helpful? What was their behavior like in our past conflicts? Etc.

We have constructed a profile of our conflict dance partner from our memories. We have developed adjectives that we have assigned to this person. These adjectives build our perceptual frame around the person. This framework takes on a reality of its own in our subjective perception of the person including those of our constructed memories. Each action or inaction of the other person re-enforces for us their 'typical' or 'personal characteristics'' that we have previously assigned to them. However, even more, each new action or inaction, changes the memory of the prior actions and inactions. These are all part of our perspective. The other person has done the same kind of framing on us.

Hence, both of us will be making decisions in these conflict situations that may have little to do with our actual prior experience. Rather we will be making decisions but based on our reconstructed memories that we now know may have little resemblance to what actually happened from both of our perspectives. Both parties are unconsciously reconstructing these memories in service of their current desired conflict outcomes that also remain largely unexamined.

Restoried and altered memories constructions are not the only flaw that can affect our perspective about our dance partner. Daniel Simon and Christopher Chabris at the University of Illinois have researched several topics related to the faultiness of our intuitions. We would like to point out one area in particular that we think has a bearing on our conflict perspective: *Inattentive Blindness.* Their research demonstrates that when people focus their attention on a demanding task, they often simply do not notice events and objects that appear in full view. They call this "inattentive blindness". In their

> We are simply not registering what we are seeing because we are not looking for it.
>
> Perhaps we might invert a familiar phrase here: "Out of mind, Out of sight".

best-known study, they asked subjects to watch a short video of group people moving around and passing a basketball back and forth. They tasked the observers with counting the number of times the basketball changed hands when passed among players wearing white. In the middle of this action, a person in a gorilla suit unexpectedly walks through the basketball passing action. Although 90% of subjects believe that would notice the gorilla, only 50% were actually able to do so. (Personally, we were one of the people who actually missed seeing the gorilla. On a second viewing, it was amazing how obvious it was but we simply did not see it. We were too focused on counting passes.) The compelling thing about Simon's and Chabris's research is that they are describing phenomena that occur at the level of our conscious perception. Our conscious perceptional bandwidth so to speak is only so wide and by focusing our attention on some things, we are bound to miss other things. More importantly, we will be unaware of what it is that we are missing.

What is the importance of this in conflict episodes? As we noted above, we have constructed a framework based on our memories of experiences with our dance partner. We have built up and reinforced this framework with each passing experience – indeed altering even the recollection of previous encounters – all adding to making the framework seem more real, solid and predicable of future behavior than it actually is. What this research suggests is that, given this framework when we interact with our conflict dance partner we may miss, *not even perceive*, and not just ignore, any unexpected behaviors. Those behaviors that disconfirm my perceptual framework may simply not register as a conscious sense perception. This creates a situation for us where it becomes increasingly hard for us to alter our perspective about our conflict dance partner and them about us. Both of us may miss behaviors that might encourage us to rebuild our framework and open up new space for more integration. What is more, even if we do pick them up, given the framework's distortion, we may misinterpret those behaviors.

Beyond our personal background, constructed memories and inattentive blindness as part of our perspective construction, our value system also forms a critical part of our conflict perspective. Values tell us what we should expect in terms of people's behavior in any given situation: what we should expect from ourselves; what we expect from the other person; by our understandings: of right and wrong, fair and unfair, of how our dance partner should act or should not act in various situations. These behavioral expectations form some of the most powerful elements of our perspective. Their power derives in no small part because they are operating below the level of consciousness as kinds of intuitions.

We bring all of these to the conflict and so does our dance partner. These become especially powerful drivers of conflicts over expected behaviors – the most common and potentially explosive kind of conflicts we have. So when Fisher and Ury advise us in *Getting to Yes* that we ought "to separate the people from the problem" we agree, but we must recognize as well that this is easier said than done.

In fact, Roger Fisher emphasizes this in his second book with Scott Brown, *Getting Together: Building Relationships as We Negotiate*. He notes that partisan perceptions can be even especially damaging in our conflict interactions. If we value cooperation, understanding, and honesty, we will undoubtedly see our own conduct as more cooperative, more understanding, and more honest than our dance partner sees it. "Likewise, if I have serious differences with you, I am likely to see your behavior as lacking these qualities."

It doesn't take much imagination to see how these differences of perspective may be fueling part or all of the conflict. All of these perceptual frameworks come into play and have a large determinant factor on how we are going to manage the conflict.

Given these deeply embedded personal perspectives, both our conflict dance partner and we will have a difficult time seeing our conflict from each other's perspective. Kenneth Thomas alerts us to what he calls our "egocentricity predicament" and its profound effect on how we manage our conflicts. *Egocentricity* means we understand the conflict issue solely in terms of our own concerns without consideration of the concerns of the other party. If we focus exclusively on our concerns, then egocentric perceptions of an issue will likely generate either/or sets of alternatives. "Either my concern is satisfied or it isn't." Beyond that, our self-absorption attentiveness tends to minimize the importance of addressing the other's concerns and to create the appearance that the other's behavior seems capricious and unreasonable. Thus, egocentric perceptions are likely to generate competitive (win-lose) intentions. This increases the likelihood that we will neither envision nor seek to find an integrative solution to our conflict.

This makes managing conflicts, especially conflicts over how we expect our dance partner to behave, difficult to deal with. This leads many people to believe that finding integrative solutions are a fantasy.

This situation may remind readers of Plato's "Allegory of the Cave". In Book VII of *The Republic*, Socrates ask Glaucon to imagine a cave where people have been imprisoned from birth. They are chained with their legs and necks locked into place so they forced to stare only at the wall in front of them. They are not able to look around at the cave, at each other, or even themselves. A fire blazes behind the prisoners but between them and the fire is a raised path with a low wall. Behind the low wall, people walk carrying objects or puppets "of men and other living things". They are walking in such a way that low wall prevents their bodies from casting shadows for the prisoners to see. However, the objects they carry are high enough that they do cast a shadow for the prisoners to see. The prisoners cannot see what is actually going on behind them, they see only shadows

> When people in a relationship are further apart – in terms of distance, culture, background and role – the contrast between their perceptions will be greater and each will find it more difficult to appreciate how the other sees things. (*Getting Together*)

cast upon the cave wall in front of them. If the prisoners only see the shadows then that is the "reality" for the prisoners because they unaware of the true nature of their perceptions. Like the Cave Dwellers, the true nature of our perceptions and the reality underneath our perceptions also remains hidden from us. In Plato's analogy, this only becomes clear to the one of the cave dwelling denizens when they break free of being chained facing the wall of shadows to discover their predicament. By raising the level of our awareness of the power of our own perceptual chains, we stand a better chance of finding more integrative solutions to our conflict situations.

As we move forward in the book, we must confront some thorny and uncomfortable questions:

- How do we go about examining our own perceptions that we bring to the situation?

- What can we do to increase our self-awareness in conflict situations?

- When the conflict occurs, how do we get at the questions of what role our perceptions and perspectives are playing in the conflict?

It seems nearly impossible to bring those questions into play at the moment the conflict actually begins. In order to examine those, we to create some kind space to reflect. What we need to be able to do is to step back from the conflict moments and reflect.

This is more likely if we don't escalate the conflict during the initial episode. If we can keep from escalating it on either our side or theirs, then perhaps we can create an opportunity to see how our perceptions are coloring the conflict. That's an important step, and one that we will need to build into our method if we are to avoid trying to get "our way" as quickly as possible. The "getting our" way egocentric mindset is what sets us up for escalation.

We need to figure out how we can take some practical steps to ask ourselves some specific and particular questions about what our perspective is. We can bring our perspective to light in a way that allows us to find ways to manage the conflict of perspectives. This also includes our emotional reactions and attachments to our perspective. These are all driven by our perception and interpretation of the situation and our dance partners.

Exercise 2: An examination of your perspective

For yourself, answer the following questions

My perspective on the situation:

1. What the conflict issue(s) is (are)
2. The conflict causes
3. Who all might be involved or affected
4. The conflict's history
5. How it began
6. Where is likely to go

My perspective about myself:

1. How is this affecting what I care about
2. What my position on the issue is.
3. What I want the conflict outcome to be.
4. What I think might be the best way(s) to get what I want.
5. What my role in the conflict is.
6. How I have been behaving in the conflict.
7. My intentions – what should I do about this?

My perspective on my dance partner:

1. What they are asking of me.
2. What is their role in the conflict.
3. What is their position on the issue.
4. What they want the conflict outcome to be.
5. Their intentions – what they should do about this?
6. How they are behaving in the conflict.

As you completed this exercise, what did you find hardest to answer?

Why? How can you improve your ability to answer those questions?

What role are these playing in your specific conflict?

Which ones are especially significant barriers to listening to and responding to the concerns of your dance partner?

What steps can you take to overcome those barriers?

Conflict Episode

Let's begin with what Ken Thomas calls the conflict episode. We will unpack the conflict episode and add some other elements to augment what Thomas suggested. We will use the episode graphic as a kind of map to guide us through much of our reflections on conflict.

Thomas writes "conflict is a process that unfolds in a series of episodes." The concept of the episode is a powerful way of understanding what happens in all conflict situations. Once we understand the process, we can anticipate what will happen in our conflict situations and make decisions that are more likely to lead to integrative outcomes.

Think of conflict episodes as the scenes of a play. Good drama is about conflict. Even the comedies are about conflict, they are just treated in different ways. The good movies are about conflict. If they're not, why would we be watching them?

If we think about our conflicts as our life's dramas, we gain some distinct advantages. First of all, it gives us a little distance on the conflict. Distance helps us relax and not stress out which is very often a problem in conflict situations. We might try thinking, "This is another little drama that I have to act in today. Of course, I'm the lead actor. There's some bit players; they have something to do, but essentially it's my drama. I am the one who needs to figure out how to play out these scenes."

We can begin to see that the conflict has a structure and dynamic to it. It is not just some hot chaotic mess of emotions and accusations. We have act one, scene one act where we become aware of the conflict issue, the main characters and the start of the plot. We can see that we can make conscious choices about what to do during the episode; just as if we are authoring the scene in a play. These choices will have a significant effect on the play's final act. It could be a one-act play if we solve the issue at the end of the first scene (episode). If not, then it's going to go through further scenes (episodes) until the issue is resolved one way or another.

So let's take a closer look at the conflict episode beginning with a quick 30,000 foot, 500 mph view. After that, we can examine each episode element and add a few things of our own to help make clear how we can apply this to help us with our day to day conflicts.

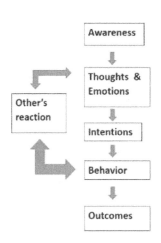

This is Thomas's basic diagram of the conflict episode. As we look at the episode, we want to see where we might intervene and how to increase our chances for the possible integrative outcome. Where if we took a particular approach would it increase my chance of having a successful outcome? Recall our caution from earlier that we are not going to be successful 100% of the time. Nothing in this guarantees we will be able to solve all of our little dramas with an integrative solution. But with a better diagnostic analysis and some practice, we will be able to increase our chances of more actual integrations as well as managing other conflicts to keep them from escalating. So with modest expectations, here we go.

We know that conflict begins with an *awareness* that the other party has done or is going to something that negative affects what we care about. To steal a phrase from Shakespeare's Henry IV, "The game is afoot." when this happens. The rest of the conflict episode unfolds from this immediate awareness of the threat to our concerns.

Once that we become aware that what we care about is being negatively affected, an emotion flashes into our consciousness – like lightening in a summer storm. This emotion is followed almost instantly – like the thunder from the lightening – by a *thought*. Since what we care about is being threatened, both the emotion and the thought are an intuitive reaction to being threatened. They just happen.

At this point, the Thomas model has us thinking about what we should do in response to this threat to what we care about – what is our *intention*. We have an opportunity to craft some kind of strategic response to this threat. Thomas posits two possible and very distinct kinds of responses: distributive and integrative.

From our intentional consideration, we act *("Behavior"* according to the episode model). Our actions are meant to put into play our intentions in accord with either the distributive or integrative response decision.

Up to this point everything that happens has taken place inside our head, once we act then the other party 'reads' our behavior. Now they have to respond to our actions. They, in turn, will form some kind of awareness, thoughts, emotions, intentions and actions of their own.

At a certain point, the episode is over (the scene ends) and we can assess the outcome of the episode in two dimensions. What has happened to the conflict issue during the episode? What has been the effect on the relationship between the two parties because of the conflict episode?

If we solved the conflict issue, then there will not be another episode for this conflict. If the issue is not resolved, then we can expect a second episode and maybe others to try to resolve the conflict issue.

That is the overview explanation of the Thomas conflict episode. Let's dive more deeply into the model and its implications.

Awareness

The conflict begins when we become aware that the other person has done or is going to do something that negatively affects what we care about. (Of course, we might have done something that negatively affects what the other person cares about. This, too triggers a conflict.) The first thing to notice is the conflict arises from awareness. Or we might say *recognition of a threat* to what we care about. This recognition/awareness is typically not a deliberative process. We are aware that reading this book and how its feel in our hands. We are aware of the temperature in the room. We are aware of the sounds in the room, perhaps of the noises drifting from the outside or the soft hiss of the steam from the radiators. None of these things results from our deliberation. So, too, in conflict situations.

If we are unaware of what the other person is doing something that threatens what we care about, then there is as of yet no conflict. Without recognition, we only have a potential conflict. We may never become aware of what they have done so it never becomes an actual conflict. They may have harmed us but no conflict resulted from the harm if we are never aware of it.

Interestingly, our brains evolved to be particularly attuned to detecting threats as a survival mechanism. Daniel Kahneman notes that a threat detected "probably traveled via a superfast neural channel that feeds directly into a part of the brain (the amygdala) that processes emotions." This had evolutionary value for early humans by shaving tenths of a second off predator recognition. The automatic instinctual responses reflect this evolutionary heritage. Kahneman remarks further that "No comparably rapid mechanism exists for recognizing good news . . . (and) threats are privileged above opportunities . . ."

There is no moral or ethical meaning attached to who first negatively affected the other party. Sometimes in our classes and workshops, learners believe that starting a conflict means that person has committed some kind of transgression. They are 'to blame' for the situation.

On the other hand, we teach that no culpability per se develops from having initiated the conflict. It may have been important that we purposely initiated the conflict as it often happens in the case of change efforts.

As we discussed earlier, the definition should draw our attention to the idea of what we "care about" being negatively affecting. The other's (or our) behavior only becomes a conflict issue if it negatively affects what we care about. If we benefit from their actions or if we don't care about 'it' then it is not a conflict for us. Hence, and this is sometimes hard for people to understand, the same behavior directed toward us which does not cause us a conflict when directed toward someone else may cause a large conflict. In the former case, we don't care about what they are doing. In the latter case, the same behavior does threaten what the other person cares about. This ought not to read as anything other than each party cares about different things. Too often, we read this as 'proof' that there is something wrong with the person who believes they were negatively affected by what we have done.

One of my favorite examples of this in a situation involving my wife and I and friend of ours. We will call him Jimmy. For whatever reason, whenever we see Jimmy, he makes it a point to gently insult me. Nothing over the top, mind you. Just some kind of smart-ass or sarcastic remark meant to rib me. I honestly could care less; I am amused. My wife on the other hand really chafes when he does this. Same person, same remark – two different sets of concerns, two different reactions. One is a conflict. One is not.

Thinking about what we care about obviously brings the whole issue of perspective into consideration. Our perspective in all of its fullness, biases and idiosyncrasies determines what we care about and the intensity of that concern. Our perspective, therefore, in a strong sense, is just as much the cause of the conflict as is the other person's behavior that arises from their perspective as well. In fact, we could make a strong case that in almost all of our conflicts, our own perspective "creates" the conflict. Recall the fullness of our earlier exploration of everything that goes into our perception and memories. Had we not cared about this, then the other person's behavior would have been of no import to us.

But the role of our perspective in the conflict episode does not end there; it is central to all aspects of the conflict episode process.

In our classes and workshops, we ask learners to think about a conflict they have had on the job. We ask them what the other person did to negatively affect what they cared about. Then, we asked what was it that they cared about that was negatively affected. We ask them to try to be a specific as possible. Here are some common responses:

- doing my job well,
- reputation,
- being trusted by others,
- being effective,
- meeting my deadlines,
- staying within budget,
- being respected,
- looking like I know what I am doing,
- being fair,
- protecting my colleagues,
- telling the truth,
- keeping the project on track,
- not wasting my time,
- being influential,
- not having to do extra work,
- my life-work balance,
- being threatened,

- being made to feel insecure,

- being held accountable,

- getting promoted,

- keeping my job,

- supporting my team,

- departmental morale,

- the stress level,

- doing the right thing,

- my organization's reputation,

- following the law,

- future job opportunities,

- looking good to my boss,

- my credibility,

- my integrity,

- my self-esteem,

- being impartial,

- being right,

- loyalty,

- safety,

- our mission,

- getting paid,

- being over worked,

- my status,

- money,

- my authority,
- being relevant,
- traditions,
- setting a precedent,

. . . (Read the list; you can add your own concerns as well as these)

We then ask. "If we made a list of all of the things you care about, how long would that list be?" Twenty items? Thirty? More? What are the chances that during the day someone you interact with is going to negatively affect one of those things? Clearly, the chances are quite high and get even higher the more people interacting with you. Flip that around. What are the chances that during the day you will negatively affect something that one of those people care about? Quite high, maybe even higher. This understanding of conflict makes it clear that conflict is ubiquitous. So when people say they avoid conflict, they are mistaken. There is no way to avoid it. It simply happens. Now what they actually mean is that they avoid responding to it. This is a common confusion; the confusion between the conflict itself and my response to it. We will have more to say about this later.

Thomas notes the research identifies three sources or types of conflict. Our awareness of being negatively affected when analyzed will fall into one or more of these three types of conflicts. Put in another way, we can group the things that people care about into three kinds of concerns. Now we know from years of experience of teaching that the way that the academic research names and describes these three is confusing if we try to apply them in practice.

We have tried to clarify those three sources. For the purpose of use in practice, these are conflicts over facts, conflicts over interests and conflicts over expected behavior. So the behaviors that negatively affect what we care about are grouped into these three categories. If our dance partner does something that we think damages our reputation, then we have a conflict over expected behavior. If our dance partner argues about when we have to complete a project, then we have a factual conflict. If we are in dispute over who how to distribute budget resources, we have an interest conflict.

CONFLICT IS THE SEA WE SWIN IN.

Let's be clear about this. The threat recognition occurs at synaptic speed – seconds or fractions of seconds. Our minds 'read' the entire context of what we are perceiving and make an instantaneous threat assessment. Only on careful reflection can we discern, analyze, deconstruct and categorize what the mind recognized immediately. In many conflict situations in which we find ourselves, it may not be immediately obvious to us exactly why we are negatively affected by what this person just said or did. We just recognize that something is amiss.

However, because deeper reflection and proper diagnosis of the conflict sources is so critical in finding the integrative space, they deserve a section their own. So we will treat these more extensively later in the book.

Emotions and thoughts

Once we become aware that what we care about is being negatively affected, an emotion flashes into our consciousness – like lightening in a summer storm. We do not choose this emotion. It is not an act of deliberation. Driven and framed by my perspective, it is an instinctual reaction to being threatened, built into our DNA. Like reading a sign on the wall, it is not something we can control. Our instinctual fight or flight response built into our DNA arises from being threatened. Which of the varietal fight or flight emotions we might experience also depends on an intuitive assessment of a number of factors. All of which also operate at synaptic speed below my level of conscious recognition. Typical emotional reactions to my awareness that what we care about are anger, fear, frustration, anxiety, irritation, disgust, feeling betrayed, hurt, disappointment, resignation, exasperation, etc. The first two, anger and fear, the Buddhists call the mind killers because our ability to think calmly, rationally and act intelligently is severely compromised in the presence of these strong emotions. Yet, unfortunately, these negative thoughts and emotions form our first subjective material from which we will be fashioning some kind of response.

This emotion is followed almost instantly – like the thunder from the lightening – by a thought. Since what we care about is being threatened, the thought, like the emotion, is an intuitive reaction to being threatened. On later reflection, we may alter our thinking, but not in the moment of recognition of threat. The thought's particular content depends on an assessment of a number of factors. All of which operate at synaptic speed below our level of conscious recognition at the moment of the original thought. The thought will be an expressional mental outburst of the flash threat calculation of those contextual factors. For example, let's say that your dance partner is a long term antagonist in a number of your conflict dramas. So, "That son of bitch", "Not again!" "Damn it, every time it's the same old shit." "Here we go again." "I should have guessed." "Well, isn't this just typical." "Screw her." Based on reports of hundreds of learners, these outbursts quite often involve profanity – not surprising when dealing with threats to what we care about. You can check your own memory for examples of this.

Now the Thomas episode model moves from *Emotions and Thoughts* to *Intention*. But in many actual conflict episodes the *Intention* phase is skipped. People move right from negative emotions and thoughts to actions or, maybe better described as, reactions. The angry reaction to threats to my concerns can range from mild irritation to sarcastic retorts to heated arguments to threats to actual physical assaults. The fearful reaction to threats to our concerns can include withdrawal from the situation, avoidance of response at all – silence, compliance and acquiescence.

In both cases, our only consideration is advancing or defending our own concerns. In the first case, we believe we have a puncher's chance of defending the concerns that our dance partner is threatening. We sense that we can win so we come out swinging. In the latter case, we intuitively recognize our dance partner is bigger, stronger, faster or higher on the food chain; we will have to move out of harm's way either literally or figuratively. In both cases, this can take place without reflection or deliberation at the level of intuition. This instinctual reaction carries me straight into the Thomas *Behavior* phase by passing intention altogether.

Intention

Let's say that we do not react immediately, but create some space or take some time to think so the Thomas intentional phase kicks in. We have to decide what we are going to do about this threat to what we care about. From our perspective, what is the mental/emotional material from which we will fashion a response? Interwoven here in complicated ways is how we perceive both the issue and the person generating the negative affect on our concerns.

As we think about the person, our memories of our past dealings with them come immediately to mind. These memories are a significant factor in forming our intentions about what to do this time. What is the state of our relationship? Have we danced on this issue before - is this another episode in our attempt to resolve the issue? How have they treated us in the past on this issue? Have they listened to us; shown any concern for our perspective? Or is this new territory for us? What is the best way to approach this person? What do we recall as successful and unsuccessful ways for us to get what we want from them? What is our perspective on how they feel about us? What frame have we built around them? What adjectives make up that frame? How does their current behavior fit that frame – typical or not?

Emotional intensity mounts a significant barrier to thinking clearly about this for both of us. What is the emotional content of those memories?

How intense are my emotions? What about their emotions?

If we have not dealt with them before, then we have nothing about them to remember. But they did may remind of others. Our memories of those former dance partners will come to mind and we will associate those memories with this person now in front of us. Think of these as "surrogate memories". We do have to make some guesses about our new dance partner. We will base those guesses on our memories of others. Whom we judge to be "just like" this person.

In addition to these considerations of past interactions, we project into the future the likelihood of other interactions and how my response might affect those events. Considerations of future exchanges with our dance partner has a way of mitigating our responses if we expect to have either frequent or significant interactions.

What about the threat itself to what we care about? How much do we care about this? This carries an emotional component of its own separate from our emotional reaction to the other person. To what degree are we able to separate the issue from the other person? As with our consideration on the other person, we may ask, is this a continuation of an issue unresolved from previous episodes? Or is it a new threat to what we care about? Do we associate it with other prior conflict issues? How much clarity do we have about this issue? Do we see it linked to other issues with this person? What do we really want? What can we realistically expect?

Beyond deliberating about how to get what we want, we might weigh the ethical considerations about the various ways we might proceed. What values should guide and constrain our actions? Once, we bring in these kind of ethical considerations, we may begin to consider the conflict event from the perspective of the other person. What does our behavior look like from their perspective? What do they care about that we, ourselves, may have already negatively affected? Is their behavior a response to something that we knowingly or unknowingly did to them? How concerned are we about what matters to them? How willing are we to make their concerns a part of our solutions to the conflict?

Like the considerations of our future interactions, these reflections offer us the opportunity to make a choice between significantly distinct solution approaches: the distributive approach and the integrative approach. We will see below how these differ, but they are born here in the intentional phase.

Behaviors

Based on how we answer (or even if we happen to entertain) these and similar kinds of questions, we will form some kind of plan of response to the threat to what we care about. On reflection, we may consider three basic possible responses. First, we may decide to do nothing. Just let it go. Perhaps, upon consideration, this really was not a threat or that much of a threat to what we care about. Or perhaps, we see this as largely a waste of time, no matter what we do, nothing will change; so why bother. Or, maybe, we are too afraid of what will happen if we do address it. Maybe we are afraid it will damage the relationship or create an emotional reaction that we don't want to deal with. Or perhaps the person will respond by retaliating against us. They are more powerful or ruthless than we are. So based on these or other fears, we choose not to get our concerns addressed.

Second, we could focus our response on getting the other person to understand our perspective on the conflict in order to protect and defend our concerns. We could plot a course to maximize the chances of winning what we want from the conflict. We can devise tactics that move the conflict settlement in our direction and away from what our dance partner is trying to achieve. We can construct arguments and compile facts that highlight the strength of our perspective's approach which at the same time show the weaknesses in our dance partner's perspective's approach. We can demonstrate why our solution to the conflict should be the preferred solution, and why our partner's solution should be rejected. We could resort to various forms of trickery in an effort to confuse or disorient them. Even if we can't get everything we want, we might be able to work out terms for a favorable compromise from our perspective. Thomas calls this the "distributive path" and we will examine it in detail below along with why and how escalations likely result from that approach.

Finally, we could respond by seeking to understand the conflict issue better from the perspective of our dance partner. We could ask questions, probe for a deeper appreciation, and develop a keener insight into their perspective on the issue and their concerns. We could open ourselves to the possibility that we might be mistaken. At a minimum, we realize that our perspective is not the only one to consider or that it is the most privileged one. Follettt and Thomas call this the "integrative path" and we will examine it in detail below along with the solution paths for the three conflict sources we mentioned above. We call this "the search for the integrative space." It lies at the heart of our approach to conflict; therefore, we will cover it in depth later.

The other person's response based on which of the three behavior's I choose

Consider for a minute that awareness, thought, emotion, and intention all occur in our head. If we have on our poker face or they are not in the direct contact with us, then up to now the other person doesn't know what we are thinking. But as soon as we act, the other person sees, hear, reads, etc. what we are doing. Now they are aware of our response - what we are saying and doing. They have a chance to now respond to our actions based on their perspective of what we have just done. What will their likely response be? Let's examine them based on our three possible responses: no response, the distributive response, the integrative response.

If for whatever reason, we choose not to respond, then our dance partner will most likely assume that whatever they are doing does not cause us a problem. Since we have said nothing, then we must be okay with what they are doing. The Latin phrase for this is, "qui tacet consentire videtur." (He who is silent is taken to agree.) More simply, we say silence implies consent. This turns out to be an unhappy realization for the conflict avoiders in all of us.

Frequently, in class and workshops, learners tell stories about avoiding to respond to conflict instances where what they care is about is being negative affected. They complain, often emotionally, that the other person continues to act in ways they find objectionable. When we ask them why they do not raise this as an issue, we get some variations on the reasons for not responding we mentioned above. They usually harbor a significant amount of ill will toward their dance partner because the dance partner continues to engage in the same behaviors that our learners deem objectionable. We typically point out to them that in such instances they are partly responsible for their own situation. Often this is not well received. On reflection, however, they realize that it is not quite fair to blame the other person when they have not made their conflict partner aware of the issue. When our learners get up the courage and use the right integrative approach, they often find a dance partner willing to talk about and sometimes to find a mutually beneficial solution.

In the instances, where we use a distributive approach and employ any number of means to induce or pressure our dance partner to see things from our perspective, we almost inevitably generate a distributive approach in return. The person 'reads' our response (where we tell them about our concerns) as not being interested in understanding the conflict issue from their perspective. This they will most often read as our negatively affecting something that they care about. They then go through the same awareness-thought-emotion-intention-behavior pattern that we did. This triggers an escalation cycle between us as each side in turn tries to get the other to see it their way. We cover this in more detail below. See the section on Distribution and Escalation.

If we take an integrative approach, we ask the other person questions that clarify the issue from their perspective. We follow up with deeper probes to gain more insight into the other person's perspective. How will they 'read' this? Highly unlikely that they will perceive this as a threat to what they care about. Hence, it does not trigger the escalation cycle. More likely, they will relax, become more cooperative and share information with us that often allows us to see potential for mutually beneficial solutions. More detailed below in the section On the Search for the Integrative Space.

Outcomes

Whenever the episode (scene) ends, we need to assess what has happened in two dimensions: what has happened to the issue, and what has happened to the relationship.

Regarding the issue, the question is have we made progress on the issue? Progress on the issue includes making the issue clearer, more specific and more detailed. It also means that both of us agree on what are the conflict issues. It does not mean we agree on the solution but that we agree on what is generating the conflict episode. (See section on The Neutral Statement of the Conflict) If we have made progress on the issue, then it is much less likely either of us will see the need to escalate the conflict. Escalating the conflict decreases the chances we can come to a mutually beneficial solution. We eliminate the feeling of frustration that we are not getting anywhere which is at the heart of the reasons to escalate the conflict in its early stages. (See Distribution and Escalation section below.)

Next we have to assess what has happened to the relationship during the conflict episode. We want the relationship to improve or at least avoid damaging it during the episode. So what kinds of things damage relationships especially at work? First, if we make judgments about the other person and/or their motives, we are bound to get resistance. No one wants to be judged. When we believe from our perspective that we are being judge, we will vigorously defend ourselves. Not listening, interrupting, arguing are also behaviors in the episode that have a likelihood of damaging the relationship. All of these show a resistance on our part to try to understand the conflict issue from their perspective.

To strengthen the relationship, we need to demonstrate that we can see things from the other person's perspective. We show our willingness to do that by asking questions about their perspective rather than making statements about our own. So suspending judgments during the episode is important when we first sit down and ask them questions. Looking at it from their point of view shows respect. If we are asking questions and asking them to explain what's going on from their perspective, we have demonstrated concern. Properly done, it signals empathy, curiosity and humility. We show them some vulnerability by revealing we don't know everything about the situation. We can learn something from their perspective by listening and asking questions.

Once we unpack this, it is clear that the best way to make both progress on the issue and maintain/improve the relationship is to ask questions and pursue an integrative strategy. Recognizing this fact should help us regulate our behavior during the episode. We need to keep checking, asking ourselves, "Are we gaining clarity on the issue? How are we doing on the relationship?"

Another episode or are we one and done

This can be a single episode or a one-act play where we resolve the issue in this episode. If the issue is not resolved then it is likely there will be other episodes that try to get the issue resolved.

If we think about the dual nature of the conflict episode outcomes, we can see how we could resolve the issue and damage the relationship. We may be able to force our solution on our dance partner without regard for their concerns through organizational power, sheer chutzpa, trickery or some other means. We can get our way but at the price of damaging the relationship. Sometimes, people in positions of authority ask, "If I have the power to solve the conflict issue to my satisfaction, why shouldn't I? After isn't that why I have the organizational authority?"

We have two answers to that question. The first is that it runs the risk of damaging the relationship with the other person. Too often people in positions of authority say that relationships are important at work and then act as if they were not important when it comes to getting what they want. We expect to work cooperatively with our subordinates over the long run. Their willingness to look out for us and help us accomplish our goals is critical to our success. Any person in a position of authority owes much (perhaps most?) of their success to the quality of the assistance from their subordinates.

Damaging those relationships is unlikely to result in open resistance or defiance. Rather, various forms of passive aggressive behaviors with plausible deniability are far more likely. Employees simply do not go beyond the bare minimum needed to keep the boss off their backs. We can think of this as wicked compliance. The least I can do to keep you off my back is the most I am going to do. The floor becomes the ceiling; the minimum becomes the maximum. People in positions of authority need to think long and hard about damaging the relationship with their subordinates if for no better reason than sheer self-interest.

Secondly, what if you're wrong? What if your intuition, experience, memory – your subjective perspective is mistaken? We know for sure that your perspective is undeniably partial. What if your organizational position itself blinds you to seeing a better way of doing things? In conflict issues, your dance partner is telling you that from their perspective you've missed something. How risky is it to override, ignore or dismiss other perspectives in conflict situations – especially when you're the boss?

It is also possible that we can maintain or improve the relationship, or at least not endanger it, by not addressing the issue. We showed above how often people simply avoid responding to a conflict out of some kind of fear.

Some other observations on the Conflict Episode

We mentioned above that if the issue is not resolved in the first episode, then it may return in future episodes in order for us to resolve it. We call that a "sequential conflict" where each episode follows the one before in a sequence of episodes over one conflict issue that remains unresolved. Sometimes these sequential episodes are planned as both parties agree to meet to work out more details to resolve the conflict. Other times unresolved issues from the initial meeting arise more spontaneously. This is a common pattern when one of the parties chooses not to avoid reacting to the conflict.

Additionally, there are "serial conflicts". These multiple conflicts are going on roughly simultaneously and in parallel over different issues but with the same conflict partner. Almost every class or workshop includes learners involved in serial conflicts. This phenomena tends to confuse people into thinking it is just a single conflict all caused by just one person. Learners tends to identify their conflict partner as some kind of problem personality that "can't get along with anyone".

While that problem personality characterization may turn out to be true, it is a mistake to lump all of the conflicts together without regard for separating out the specific conflict issue in each case. If we do not break them apart and analyze each conflict issue in its individual particularity, then we will not be able to gain clarity on any of the issues. Without that clarity, we will have a very difficult time finding mutually beneficial solutions to any of these conflict issues. We will be reduced to simply complaining about what a pain in the ass our dance partner is. Which while it may be true, does not bring us any closer to finding a mutually beneficial solution.

After this section's Exercise, we will delve into the three kinds of conflicts that launch our awareness that our concerns are being threatened.

Exercise 3 Restorying using the model

Retell your story using the conflict episode model.

Awareness – briefly describe the circumstances when you first became aware that what you cared about was being negatively affected by your dance partner

Thought – what did you think when that happened

Emotions - name the emotion(s) you felt at the time

Intention – when you thought about what you should do about this, what kind of things did you consider? What was the most important thing that you thought you needed to do?

Behavior – what actions did you take in response to this threat to what you cared about? What did you say to your dance partner?

Their reaction – When you took those actions, how did your dance partner respond? What did they say and do?

Outcome – How did the episode end? What was the effect on the conflict issue; what was the effect on the relationship with your dance partner as a result of this episode.

Types of Conflict

Thomas's research revealed three sources or types of conflict: judgment conflicts, goal conflicts and normative conflicts. As we said before, these terms and their descriptions tend to confuse practitioners making it harder for them to apply in practice. We have changed these to factual conflicts, interest conflicts and behavioral expectation conflicts. Our conflicts can be any combination of all three. It can begin as one kind of conflict and evolve into a second type. We can resolve one type only to find another has emerged from that resolution. In his meta-review of the conflict literature, the types of conflict take up very little attention or space in Thomas' article.

In practice, however, being able to analyze the types of conflicts active in our conflict is a critical diagnostic step. What makes it so critical to analyze each type is that each type requires a different approach to manage. We call those approaches "solution paths". These conflict solution paths are distinct from each other. Three types equals three different approaches to management and possible resolution. This gives us a powerful tool in keeping both parties focused on the conflict issue.

First, we can much more quickly zero in on the specific kind of conflict and initiate the first steps down the solution path. We know from the escalation research that the longer it takes to make progress on the conflict issue, the more likely the conflict will escalate. We will examine how this happens in the section on Distribution and Escalation.

Second, when we can identify the type(s) of conflict for our dance partner and suggest a reasonable solution path, we increase their confidence that we can find an integrative solution. Increased confidence in finding an integrative solution improves the chance that we can actually find one. If we don't believe it is possible, then we won't try and we will revert to distributive tactics to get as much as we can from the situation.

Third, the solution paths offer us a methodological approach to managing the conflict that keeps both parties working on the issue in a way that will likely make the conflict more manageable. As the parties work on the issue and make progress, they are less likely to turn their attention to each other as the source of the conflict. This helps keep the separation between the issue and the person and increases the potential for an integrative solution.

Fourth, following the theme of separating the person and the issue, very often we identify 'the person' as the problem. Similarly, we are likely to think that we have "personality conflict" with the strong implication that our dance partner is the one who possesses a problematic personality. When we have a more powerful analytic tool to identify the conflict issue, we draw attention away from the "personality" explanation. We do recognize that our dance partner has a significant effect on how we manage the conflict, but, as we pointed out earlier, their response to the conflict is not the conflict itself. Their personality is not the conflict issue, what they are saying and doing is.

It is surprising how seldom the popular literature on managing conflicts fails to recognize the distinction among types of conflicts. Consequently, often the prescriptions for how to manage the conflict lack diagnostic specificity. Lack of diagnostic specificity results in prescriptions that do not target the issue as quickly and effectively as they could. Generic exhortations to be "more reasonable", "listen carefully", "try to find a way to compromise" come off as expert advice. It is not that these are bad suggestions, but they do not constitute a method of identifying the kinds of conflicts and their specific solution paths.

Let's explore the three types of conflicts in some detail. Later when we are elucidating the search for the integrative space, we will describe each one's specific solution path.

Factual Conflicts

Thomas identifies one of three sources or types of conflicts as

Judgment conflicts involve differences over empirical or factual issues. These conflicts have also been called *cognitive conflicts* . . . Here, the party perceives that the other has drawn different (incorrect) conclusions about what is true in an empirical sense. . . Judgment conflicts or controversies play a prominent role in a number of decision-making models.

We have found that identifying these kinds of conflicts as cognitive or judgment conflicts confuses the practitioners we teach and coach. People use the words judging or judgment in a variety of ways often in discussing all three sources of conflict.

We call them "Factual Conflicts". Additionally, Thomas defining them, as ". . . the party perceives that the other has drawn different (incorrect) conclusions about what is true in an empirical sense" makes it difficult for most people to grasp. So we have had to evolve others ways to get the concept across. (For ease of understanding, we assume a simple either/or answer is the case in all of my examples. It could turn out in some of them that both parties are wrong.) Here are two alternate formulations that have gained some traction.

1) Factual conflicts are disagreements over the *facts of the case*. Each of the parties is making *a factual claim*. The parties disagree as to whose factual claim is correct.

2) Factual conflicts are disputes about what is the right answer to "the question". *Both parties have an opinion about the right answer.* These opinions are not the same.

It turns out that two linguistic practices still confuse people who are trying to understand factual conflicts. First, all conflicts involve some facts. Some people have a hard time differentiating the facts *within the conflict* from the *conflict being over the facts* themselves.

For example, Dave might say, "It is a fact that this conflict involves several people."

The way past this confusion is to ask Dave, "Do you and your dance partner disagree about this?"

Dave, "No, we agree that many people are involved in the conflict."

Then, "If you agree about this, then the number of people involved is not the conflict issue and therefore this is not a conflict over these facts. The number of people involved is simply one fact among many in the conflict. However, that does not make it a factual conflict. What is that you and your dance partner disagree about?"

The second confusion comes as people raise the common distinction between facts and opinions.

For example due to her strong perspective biases, Mary asserts, "Sue has an opinion about the costs but I have the facts."

The way past this confusion is to get Mary to understand they both have opinions:

"Mary, let's sort this out. Her opinion is that the cost will be $10,000. Your opinion is that it will be closer to $15,000. She says $10,000; you say $15,000. Is that right?

Mary, "Yes. But I know I am right."

"Perhaps. When we answer the question, "How much does this cost?", then we will see that one of you will have a correct opinion and the other an incorrect opinion. We wouldn't know which is which until we resolve the conflict."

Both people have opinions. One will turn out to hold the correct opinion.

Speaking of examples, we use several different kinds of examples to help people grasp and apply the concept of a factual conflict. A fun example comes from the Dead Parrot skit by Monty Python. A disgruntled customer played by John Cleese argues with the pet shop owner played by Michael Palin about whether or not a parrot Cleese just purchased is dead. There ensues a series of hilarious attempts by each to argue, present evidence for their opinions. They each have opinions; Cleese has the correct one.

The movie *Twelve Angry Men* actually revolves around a number of fine examples of factual conflicts within the larger factual question - was the boy guilty of killing his father. If you wanted one place to go to view many factual conflicts, this movie would be the place. The scene that we use often is the dispute over the question of whether or not the old man who lived upstairs could have gotten out of bed in the time he said to see the accused running out of the apartment after stabbing his father. The reason we like to show that one is for the ingenious way they try to answer the factual question.

The third example, another fun one that centers on linguistic confusions, is the Abbot and Costello classic, "Who's on first?"

Examples for our own experiences include:

"I say you were warned about this before; you say I never warned you." (An example of a factual conflict in the past.)

"You say your commission check is in error; I say your commission check is accurate." (An example of a factual conflict in the present.)

'You say my solution will not fix the problem, I say it will." (An example of factual conflict in the future.)

In helping our learners to understand these examples, we point out to them, whether you were warned or not is a matter of fact. Either your check is accurate or it isn't, that is a matter of fact. Either my solution will work or not, that is a matter of fact.

The idea of a factual conflict about the future also puzzles some learners. "How can we have a factual conflict about something that has not happened yet?" is the common question. The answer is that both parties are making a *factual claim about what will happen* in the future. One of the parties will turn out to have made a correct claim and the other party will turn out to have made an incorrect claim. We won't know which is which for sure until that future event has taken place. Factual conflicts about the future are quite common in organizational setting. The following workplace examples are likely to generate factual dispute about the future:

What will be the results in the improvements in processes we should make?

What are our competitors planning to do?

Where we should locate a new facility?

Who should head the new department?

What are the chances that an economic downturn will occur?

In short, any time that anyone disputes over the possible future outcomes of any action we are contemplating, we will have factual conflicts. Turns out, this is quite common and can be difficult to resolve. Think about all change efforts. They are launched on the assumption that they will succeed and the results envisioned will be superior to the status quo. We have all been through these change initiatives. We know there is always resistance to them. In many cases, this opposition can be based on a factual disagreement over the likely results of these change efforts. (Interest conflicts also play a crucial role here as well.) These are critical to resolve as well since the future surviving and thriving of our organizations depend on resolving these questions.

To combine our earlier observations about perspectives with factual conflicts, we often provide a short in-class demonstration using a Coke bottle. It goes something like this.

"Okay Simon I am going to ask a question. Now don't freelance on me. Just want you to answer. So don't be making stuff up. Okay, what is what you see?

The nutritional facts, congratulations. Good job. What kinds of things are we seeing here on that listing? Fat, Sodium, Protein. Yes, very good. Are you sure absolutely certain? Is there any way I can argue you out of this? I'm really good at arguing. Yes, yes. You are definitely looking at the nutritional facts. Certain? No way to argue out of it. Good I am impressed by your confidence in what you see. Absolutely certain, bet your monthly paycheck? You would. Cool. Thank you very much.

(Moving to the next person)

Now John same instructions as I gave to Simon. John, tell us exactly what you see here. Just what you can directly observe.

An emblem? Hmmm…I think "emblem" is an interpretation. John, what do you actually see? John, right, the words Coca-Cola, Zero, Zero Calorie Coke. Excellent. John, do you notice any nutritional facts? None? Are you sure? Simon was willing to bet a month's pay he saw the nutritional facts. Hell, John, he even named some. Hmmm, what do you think? Maybe Simon's on drugs? He is seeing things that aren't there. Did he say anything about the Coca-Cola label or other words? No, he did not and you didn't see any nutritional label. John, how certain are you about what you have seen? Could we argue you out of it? I didn't think so. Bet a month's pay? Great job.

Okay Barb your turn. Tilt your head back, look up at the ceiling. I promise not to hurt you or spill anything on you. Very good.

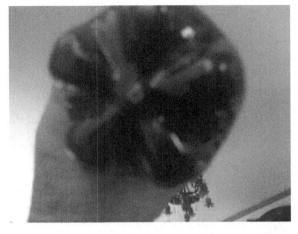

Ready? Tell me just what you see. Don't guess. Don't interpret. Just tell me exactly what you see. Yes, good. You see some kind of dark stuff contained in a round bumpy thing. Well described, Barb. Do you see any logos or any words about Coke Zero? Anything about nutrition information? Are you sure? Defend your view with vigorous arguments? Great. I don't doubt you could hold your own.

What if you were inside the bottle? Your feet would be wet and there'd be a light at the top. Is everybody mistaken? Nope. Who's right? They all are? Yes. How can that be? Exactly. Their perspectives changed; different angles means a different view. One that we would argue vehemently to defend. One from our perspective is seemingly indisputable. We can emphasize the facts, insist with utter confidence that we are right and, therefore, the other person **must be** wrong. We view these situations as either/or. The better approach is both/and.

We can insist that we have the facts and those facts allow us to solve the problem, but the lesson here is that it may not. It may not because we might be looking at it from a different angle, from a different perspective than our dance partner. Hence we can have *seeming contradictory* facts and we can both be right.

As we began this book by showing, there's a lot of evidence out there for our inability to perceive, remember, and repeat accurately what we see. Eyewitnesses are certain they saw you commit the crime. James absolutely picked you out of a lineup completely certain you did it. We get later DNA evidence shows it was not you but somebody else, even then, James may not believe he was mistaken. We may be certain, totally convinced that we are right. (We have a friend who found out when he got his birth certificate for his passport that what he thought was his first name was not actually his first name, it was his middle name. His parents never told him.) Nonetheless, we have to be careful here perspective matters even saying that we are right. These are still factual questions generating factual conflicts. What we need to keep in mind is the role of perspective in describing and framing our factual conflicts. Depending on our perspectives, we could all be right!

Behavioral Expectation Conflicts

Thomas calls the second type of conflicts 'normative' conflicts.

Normative conflicts center on a party's evaluation of another party's behavior in terms of expectations of how the other *should* behave. These expectations may involve various kinds of standards regarding proper behavior: for example, ethics ... notions of equity . . . justice . . . observance of status hierarchies . . . and various other norms of the social system. . . formal rules . . . When the party perceives a violation of these standards, such emotional reactions as disapproval, blame, and anger may be triggered, as well as sanctions intended to produce conformity to the standard.

For purposes of clarity, we refer to these conflicts as Behavioral Expectation Conflicts. They arise from our belief that the other person *should have behaved differently* than they did. Or flipping it, our dance partner expected us to behave differently than we did. The key word, "should", signals that we have a Behavioral Expectation Conflict. We use "should" when we when we wish to indicate that there is an obligation of some sort to act in a particular way. The person ought to do something; or they have a duty to do something. We also sometimes use the phrase "supposed to" to indicate what we expect of others.

Our expectations about proper or appropriate behaviors are deeply embedded in our perspectives. For the most part, they were formed early in life based on all of those factors we noted in the section on perspective. These prescribed behaviors may also arise from organizational sources – both formal i.e. legal requirements, company rules/policies/procedures and informal cultural practices "that's just the way we do things here". For the most part, we do not examine our expectations about how people ought to behave in certain situations. These unquestioned beliefs operate at an intuitive level. We react instinctively and almost immediately to other people's violations of our deeply embedded expectations.

This explains why, as Thomas suggests, such violations of our expectations trigger strong negative emotional responses. Such transgressions of our deeply held expectations undermine our confidence in the predictability of our social reality. This creates a degree of uncertainty that is likely to evoke one of our two most primary emotional response of anger or fear.

However, there appears to be something else going on in these cases. Often we find ourselves involved in conflicts over what people have simply said. On the surface, it appears that just having someone say this should not really threaten us. Yet, it does. We read these words as symbols of attacks on people, things or beliefs from our perspective. Kahneman notes in *Thinking Fast and Slow* that,

The brain responds quickly even to purely symbolic threats. Emotionally loaded words quickly attract attention, and bad words . . .attract attention faster than do happy words . . . There is no real threat, but the reminder of a bad event *(real or potential – my insertion)* is treated in System 1 as threatening. . . . The sensitivity to threats extends to the processing of statements of opinions with which we strongly disagree.

When this happens, we can no longer depend on intuitive predicable patterns of behavior. We now have to slow down and evaluate, perhaps even re-configure our own social constructions. This unexpected behavior from others is largely unwelcomed because it challenges our own expectations by exposing our beliefs as subjective, relative and perhaps even mistaken.

This, then, is the deeper threat to what we care about that turns these into conflict situations. It makes them more personal, emotional and difficult to manage properly. Separating the person from the problem is not too difficult to do in factual or interest conflicts. In these behavioral expectation conflicts, we find it difficult to believe that the person is not the problem. After all, they are clearly not acting as they should. We quickly assume that there is something fundamentally wrong with them.

We have found that a simple diagram helps people to understand and easily apply this diagnostic distinction. This accurately depicts Behavioral Expectation Conflicts. A situation arises – call it S1. Our dance partner responds to that S1 situation by deciding to act in a particular way – call it D1.

S1 = D1

When we become aware that our dance partner has done this, it negatively affects what we care about. From our perspective, they *should have* done D2 not D1.

S1 = D2

How often during our day does this happen? How often during the day do we, from our perspective, think people *should* act differently than they are? Yes, very often. How often during the day do other people, from their perspectives, think that we should have act differently than we are? Yes, very often. This means that these behavioral expectation conflicts swirl around us daily.

As we suggested above, when this happens, when someone doesn't do something we think they should or does (or says) something that we find objectionable, we automatically think that 1) they are wrong and 2) this is evidence they suffer from some kind of character flaw. It is nearly impossible not to make it about them rather than the issue. Finding a solution path that does not trigger an escalation is difficult to do. Even as we recognize what is going on, the urge to criticize and judge can overwhelm our best intentions here.

Interest Conflicts

The third type of conflict Thomas calls Goal Conflicts:

Goal conflicts involve divergent or apparently incompatible ends desired by the parties. These goals may, for example, take the form of satisfying personal needs, achieving delegated responsibilities or objectives, or obtaining scarce resources. Goal conflicts are prominent in negotiation models, where they are commonly called *interest conflicts* . . . Here, each party's pursuit of his or her own goals threatens or obstructs the goal attainment of the other . . .

Following the negotiation models, we use the term Interest Conflicts rather than Goal Conflicts. Interest Conflicts arise from our perception or our dance partner's perception that we are seeking obstructive or incompatible interests. Obstructive or incompatible means that if we get what we want, then our conflict partner cannot get what they want. Often people confuse different interests with incompatible interests. We can have different interests that are compatible. In fact, as we shall see later, finding the compatibility of different interests can create integrative space and leads to resolution of interest conflicts with both parties benefit without compromising.

Any zero-sum situation where if one party gets more, then the other party gets less provides an instance of Interest Conflict. Wikipedia defines zero-sum as:

In game theory and economic theory, a zero-sum game is a mathematical representation of a situation in which each participant's gain or loss . . . is exactly balanced by the losses or gains . . . of the other participants. If the total gains of the participants are added up and the total losses are subtracted, they will sum to zero.

So for example, poker is a zero sum situation. The winning payout, the size of the pot, is a fixed sum or zero sum. Our winnings in poker come from the other player's losses. Their winnings come from our losses. The net result of subtracting losses from winnings is zero.

Sometimes we use a pie or cake as an example of interest conflict situation. If we get a bigger piece then, you get a smaller piece and vice versa. Any fixed sum situation generates an interest conflict if both parties lay claim to the sum. Or put it slightly different, any situation where it looks like we would benefit at your expense, or you would benefit at our expense creates the appearance of an interest conflict.

The *appearance* of interest conflicts where it seems neither parties can't get what they want without the other party suffering a loss is quite common. The actual occurrence of situations where the outcome is fixed or set is much less common. Once we analyze the situation, we can see that what at first appeared to be incompatible interests turns out to be incompatible positions. We will explore that in some detail below. Nonetheless, *because our interests initially appear to be incompatible,* we call these interest conflicts.

> *Interest conflicts present us with either/or, win-lose outcomes. Set up this way, they are inherently distributive.*

In organizational situations, typical examples that generate perceived interest conflicts are

- Distribution of budget allocations – The Budget Committee announces it will award an additional $300,000 to the department that can demonstrate they will increase long term sustainable new income results. Your department along with Engineering submitted a proposal. Only one depart can win the bid.

- Budget cuts – The ever active Budget Committee announces that either your department or Marketing will lose $200,000 based on the results of an audit of the effectiveness of your operation.

- Promotions – You and Steve both apply for the job of comptroller. There is only one opening.

- Office space – Frank is retiring. He has a plum office location. You have coveted his office space for years. It turns out that John has said at the last minute that he wants it too. Now what?

- Staff assignments – Alice expects to be assigned as the representative for long-term employees to the Compensation Committee. She learns that four other senior employees are also asking to be selected for the single opening.

- Territorial sales alignments – Cindy and Teresa are the two candidates for the sales representatives in the newly created and potentially lucrative sales area.

- Customer accounts – ShowMeMoney is the hottest key customer account to be landed in years. You played a key role in landing it. Now you find out that Barb has been tagged as the Key Account Manager.

- Project management changes – Harry, the department supervisor, held a meeting to announce that new software is being installed that will increase the number of task your area will be assigned.

- Lean changes – because of the last Kaizen event, three people from your area will transferred to another department.

- Layoffs – A downturn in the demand for your aluminum pipes means that the company will lay-off 10 people.

Exercise 4 – Identifying the types of conflict in your conflict story

Based in the description and examples of the three kinds of conflict – factual, behavioral expectation and interest – do an analysis of your conflict. Describe and explain the types of conflicts present in your conflict. If one of the types of conflicts is not present, explain how you know it lacks that kind of conflict.

Factual Conflicts:

Interest Conflicts:

Behavioral Expectation Conflicts:

D istribution

We want to examine our intention to respond to the threat to what we care about in more detail. Following Thomas, we have said there are two basic paths – the distributive path and the integrative path. The distinguishing characteristic between the two is the degree to which we are willing to consider and address the concerns of our conflict dance partner. That's the critical question. If we are not interested or willing to address the other person's concerns, then we will follow a strategy of distribution – a solution path that tries to maximize getting our concerns addressed. If, on the other the other hand, we consider and address the concerns of our dance partner, then we will search for an integrative solution – one that attempts to combine their concerns and our concerns into a single solution.

The words and action we use to respond to the threat to what we care about reveal our mindset about whether the kind of response will be distributive or integrative. These actions flow from our deliberation (or lack of deliberation) about our choices. Our choices here have significant effect on the likely course of the conflict so we need to explore the consequences of each approach carefully.

All right, let's start with distribution. This is our normal approach. So let's locate the topic on our episode map.

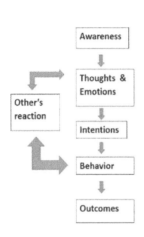

As Thomas lays this out, the conflict begins when we awareness that the other person has negatively affected what we care about. This threat to what we care about triggers certain negative emotions and thoughts regarding what they have done. Now we have to decide how we intend to respond to this threat.

Coming out of intention, we act (Behavior). In this section, we will follow the actions of distribution path. First, because that is the path we take most of the time. It's the most normal path. It's the organic path. It's the DNA path. It's the instinctual path. It's the path that we take without even thinking about it. It is what Daniel Kahneman calls a System 1 approach in his book, *Thinking Fast and Slow.*

Following our normal way of responding, typically, we will merely react without any deliberation about choices (purely System 1) or we will choose actions and behaviors that maximize the opportunities to address my concerns, specifically the ones that are being negatively affected by the other person's actions. Our reflections on what to do, Kahnamen's System 2, build a rational façade to support my intuitive reactions. As George Harrison wrote, "I, me, mine" surface as the most relevant consideration in these deliberations.

Both of these responses take us down the distributive path, but in the explanation that follows, we will lay out examples of the more deliberative approach. We think it is obvious what happens when there is no space between our negative thoughts and emotions and our actions. If not, take a visit to your local jail.

If we decide to advance or protect our threatened concerns – a perfectly natural response, we reason that we need to make our dance partner aware of what their actions doing to us. We will act in ways that maximize the chances that we will get our concerns and interests addressed. We might do this in a couple of ways but regardless we will choose tactics to get this done – to make them aware of our perspective, to protect our concerns, to defend our interests, to assert our view of reality, to promote our values.

Actuating this strategy comes down to a simple choice as we think about what we should do about this threat. As we indicated above, in some sense, it is not a conscious choice. Even as we deliberate, we are likely merely deliberating about how to activate and justify our instinctual response. Rarely, do we question this instinctual response. So as we come out of this intention phase ready to act, our first act is to make statements about our concerns. Most simply, we *tell* our dance partner what we think they need to know or what they need to do *to get our concerns addressed.* Many variations suggest themselves here. We might direct them to act in a certain way, tell them to do something or stop doing something. We could advise them what actions they need to do. We could inform them that they're wrong or mistaken or misguided or worse. We could lecture them about how to correct their errors.

We could do it nicely or aggressively:

"Listen, Denise, here's what I need you to appreciate. It's important that understand why you need to change your approach to the suppliers."

"All right, I know this is hard to do, but you really don't have a lot of choice here. The way we have to do this can never be changed."

"I'm going to make it perfectly clear to you about how we're going to do this and I know you have a certain way of doing things but it really doesn't apply here. We're going to do things differently here. Here's what I need you to do."

"Stop. Do not pass go. Do not expect to collect $200."

Now we are aware that some people advise that if we use "I statements" rather than "You statements" it makes discussion go better. In this case, we disagree. We have been around long enough to understand that in these moment, our dance partner will most likely read "I statements" as still a threat to their concerns simply because we are still focused on ourselves. No matter whether we use I-statements or You-statements, we are *still telling* them about *our* concerns, *our* perspective on the issue and *our* perspective on their behavior. That is what will most likely trigger the escalation cycle.

As we said before, this *telling response* is perfectly normal and understandable because our interests and concerns have been threatened. From our perspective, evidently they don't get this. So we're going to enlighten then about our perspective at this point.

And if we look at the episode map, we can see that by telling about our concerns, we now have acted. Our dance partner has now seen and heard us act. At this point, they become aware that we are telling them, in whatever manner that we chose, that they need to see things from our perspective. We have emphasized our concerns to the exclusion of theirs.

What is their most likely reaction to this? Most likely, at this point, since we have focused on our concerns, they will read this as either disinterest or even hostility to their own concerns. Hence, their intuitive response will be to see this as something that negatively affects what they cared about. They will likely think "Well obviously, Randy does not understand the issue and how it affects me. I need to make that more clear to him!"

Yes, so here begins their awareness that we are causing a conflict for them and their need to respond to that threat to what they care about. They have a certain thought and emotion. Will it be a happy thought and happy emotion? No. Now, they have to decide what to do about this. Most likely, they will make the same kind of choice that we did.

They will *tell us* things designed to be make us understand the issue from their point of view trying to maximize getting their concerns addressed.

"Well, Randy, here's what you don't understand. Here is what you don't get. Let me make clear to you why you are wrong (or mistaken or misinformed or misguided or) . . ."

They will repeat the same intuitive response process that we did when we became aware that our concerns were being threatened. Maybe they do it nicely, or not.

So now we hear their response. "What?!" They have paid no positive attention to what we told them. We heard what they said and we think, "Were they not listening? Where did they mention the stuff that we talked about? They didn't get it. We need to repeat ourselves. Now perhaps they're little hard of hearing? Maybe we need to repeat ourselves a bit louder. So we repeat ourselves and say something like, 'Unfortunately you weren't listening. You need to listen to me when I tell you what's supposed to happen. Are you ready to listen to me?'"

We read this as the problem they are not listening to us. We feel we have to tell them things over again to get our perspective across. So we repeat ourselves.

Yes, we tell them this or something like it. What do they do? They repeat themselves and tell us the same things from their perspective that evidently we did not listen to or understand or care about their concerns.

How many conversations have we had where we're repeating ourselves to them, three and four times and they're repeating themselves to us three or four times? Lots of times, right? And around and around we go. We call this the escalation cycle. We and our numerous dance partners have been trapped in the escalation cycle. We've experienced it both giving and getting and then giving back again.

After Exercise 5, we will expand our understanding of the role escalation plays in our conflict episodes. We need to be especially attentive to how each parties' perspective fuels the escalation when we pursue distributive approaches.

Exercise 5: The distributive path in your story

What was your response to the threat to what you cared about?

What did you say to your dance partner once you were aware of the conflict?

What you statements did you make?

What was their response?

Conflict Escalation

The driving force of the escalation cycle arises from *telling about things from our perspective* as a response to a threat to what we care about. We come out of the intention phase and we make statements about ourselves and our concerns. Now we can do this harshly or nicely, but in the end, it amounts to the same thing. Just takes a little longer if we're nice about it. Both sides feel frustrated that despite their best efforts to make the other side understand their perspective and concerns, they are not getting their concerns addressed. What will happened as a result of this cycle is that it will likely result in a series of conflict escalations.

The escalation cycle once begun takes on a life if its own. Let's explore that through the research of Friedrich Glasl's from his book *Konfliktmanagement. Ein Handbuch für Führungskräfte, Beraterinnen und Berater, (Conflict management. A guide for Executives, Consultants).* Unfortunately, Glasl's book has not been translated and my German is limited to ordering bier and schnitzel, Kann ich etwas Bier und Schnitzel haben?

Fortunately, Thomas Jordan has done a fine job of bringing Glasl's work to English readers with his article "Glasl's Nine-Stage Model of Conflict Escalation: A Summary." While Glasl's analysis covers nine stages, the final five stages are less relevant to most ordinary interpersonal organizational conflicts. So we will explore just the first four. In promoting the use of Glasl's model, Jordan remarks that Glasl's escalation model can be a useful conflict diagnostic tool. He notes that it has value as a means for sensitizing people to how conflicts escalate. Learning about the steps that one should take care to avoid helps us prevent a conflict from escalating out of control. The model also demonstrates how situational pressures acting upon people involved in a conflict can get out of control. The model makes clear the internal logic of conflict relationships, arising from the failure of "benign" ways of handling contradictory perspectives and standpoints. Without our making a conscious efforts to resist the escalation mechanisms, conflicts having a momentum of their own that inevitably leads to an escalation.

The four stages are:

1. Hardening
2. Debates and Polemics
3. Actions not Words
4. Images and Coalitions

Note that Glasl's escalation stages represent degrees of conflict harshness in ascending order marked by increases in intensity of negative emotion, a widening of the scope of the issue and pursuing more severe tactics in attempting to 'win' the conflict. Increases in the intensity of emotion tend to be frustration, anger, anxiety, and/or fear. Widening the scope of the issue means that one or both parties raise other issues beyond the original triggering issue of the conflict. Each brings in other matters in order to put pressure on the other party by trying to demonstrate a pattern of disruptive behavior. Severity of tactic means that actions are taken that increase the pressure and stress on the other party to relent or give up.

While our conflict possibly could pass through them sequentially, it need not do so. Our response to actions that threaten what we care about can begin at any of these stages. So for example, we have been heard many stories where people were unaware that they had negatively affected what someone cared about and their response was not to talk to them at all but to go right to their boss about their transgressions – Stage 3 Action not Words. We have also witnessed conflicts that went right to Stage Four with a public attack before people even became aware that they had caused a conflict.

At Stage One (Hardening), the conflict that arises between ourselves and our dance partner proves resistant to our initial efforts to resolve it. Primarily, because as we indicated above in describing the conflict escalation cycle, both of us are trying to get the other person to see it from each of their perspectives. As the arguments moves back and forth, our positions begin to harden, and we become less empathetic, more insistent on being 'right'. If we have a strong need for their cooperation in solving the issue, our frustration will rise because we cannot resolve the issue to our satisfaction without the other person helping us.

Even though, our frustration is rising, at this stage of the conflict, both of us are still committed to working together to resolve the issue. The issue remains front and center in the dispute. We are trying to deal with each other in a straightforward way. We may complain to others but we are not trying to build any kind of coalition to side with us. We are just complaining, might even ask for some advice.

The emotional level at this stage can range from cool, even amused, to fairly heated including our dance partner and ourselves raising our voices during some spirited arguments. Depending on how we remember prior incidents with them, we will quickly form an opinion about how willing or helpful they are. In any case the longer this goes on, the more likely we perceive them as being stubborn and unreasonable. And they would likely view us the same in return. We may remain at this stage of the conflict indefinitely especially if there is no outside organization pressure to resolve the issue or need to meet some kind of deadline. Many conflicts never move beyond this stage. In these instances, we will have periodic conflict episodes (sequential conflict) because the issue has not yet been resolved, each of us hoping that we can somehow convince the other person to see it our way.

At this stage, the conflict can end in one of four ways.

First, we may give up on the issue, simply relent out of weariness and frustration. We just stop trying to get a resolution to our conflict. In which case, we will not get the threat to what we care about addressed.

Second, we may find a compromise solution where we give up something of what we wanted in order to get the other person to finally cooperate and give us part of what we wanted.

Third, it is possible, that we or they may have some kind of integrative epiphany and break into the integrative space. We might each reach a level where it becomes obvious the only way to get what we what is to help our dance partner get what they want.

Fourth, we might escalate the conflict to the next stage. This escalation may either be deliberately planned or it may simply be our intuitive reactive response to building frustration over an issue we can neither leave alone nor compromise to solve.

The conflict can enter Stage Two (Debates and Polemics) either as a natural evolution from unresolved issues from Stage One (described directly above) or one of us can begin our response to the conflict directly at this level of escalation. At this stage, we judge (explicitly or intuitively) either as a result of having passed through Stage One with our dance partner, or based on our memory of past experiences with them, that they are not amenable to reason and sensible solutions. We need to be more aggressive about getting our way in this conflict. We still mostly focus on the issue but since we no longer believe our dance partner responds to reasoned arguments or clear facts, we become more confrontational, argumentative. We lock down hard on our positions, quickly dismiss theirs, trying to give the impression of strength and solid conviction.

While the conflict issue is still present in this stage, since focusing just on it seems unlikely to resolve the conflict, we begin shifting attention away from the issue per se to pressuring our dance partner. The pressure comes not from stressing the merits of issue but from finding ways to score points against them in arguments. We look for ways to make them look weak or indecisive or ill-informed or self-centered or stubborn. We create an impression that they are not to be taken seriously about this issue (and perhaps by implication anything else).

This often includes using what traditionally has been known as logical fallacies such as appealing to authorities/tradition to make me look more legitimate, attacking them personally by calling into question their motives or showing that carried out to its logical conclusion what they want is absurd. We may resort to bullying or blustering. We can also blur the issue by linking it to other issues or more amorphous global concerns. What was or could have been a search for a genuine solution to the issue has been transformed into a set of verbal tricks and maneuvers to keep our dance partner off balance and intimidated in order to get them to give in to our positions. This has the consequence of undermining the trust between us and our dance partner. They can no longer be sure about what we might do to win. They no longer see us as a reliable partner in solving this problem. Furthermore, we are creating memories of these encounters that will have a serious effect on future exchanges with our dance partner.

While it is still possible at this stage for us to work out a solution, there is still a glimmer of hope for cooperation, that glimmer is flickering. As with Stage One, this can also end in one of four ways: one of us giving in or giving up, a compromise solution, integrative epiphany or further escalation to Stage Three. Before we move on to Stage Three, I want to make three observations.

First, it is possible for one party to be in one stage and the other party to be at a different stage of the conflict since the stages are descriptions of the actions of each. So for example, my dance partner could be exhibiting actions typical of Stage One and I could be exhibiting those of Stage Two. The point here is not necessarily to decipher and categorize the stage per se but to be clear about what each party is doing and the effect it is having on both the clarity of the issue and quality of the relationship.

Second, it is important to recognize that the essence of escalation is the movement away from resolving the issue toward isolating or removing our dance partners. As we seek to gain clarity on our own actions and those of others, we need to constantly evaluate them in terms of both issue and relationship. Escalation occurs when we drift away from the issue and turn our focus on the other person. Fisher and Ury in *Getting to Yes* urge us to separate the problem from the person and to be hard on the problem and easy on the person. Glasl's research re-enforces that point because when we don't make that separation and stay focused on the issue/problem then conflicts escalate.

Third, escalation has a momentum of its own carried forward by the interpersonal dynamics of the threat to what people care about in conflict situations. This is why we often experience conflicts as kinds of runaway events that get out of hand quickly. It can be that no one really intended for that to happen but before we realized it the conflict had escalated and created more problems. This is also a good indicator of just how much of this is activated below the level of consciousness as instinctual responses to perceived threats. This means that we have to actively work so that we stop the natural momentum of escalation before it starts. In practice that means identifying the conflict issue as quickly and as specifically as possible, making sure that both parties recognize and agree on the conflict issue and that we make progress on that issue immediately. We do not have to resolve it but we have to get some progress on it so that we diminish the chances of frustration leading to escalation. As you will see moving forward in the book, our methods are specifically designed to try to increase our chances of doing just that.

In Stage Three (Actions not Words), what essentially happens is that we abandon our dance partner in resolving the conflict. Out of the frustration of dealing with them in one or both of the earlier stages, we decide talking with them is getting us nowhere. Or we believe based on past memories or surrogate memories that dealing with this person or 'these kind of people' is a waste of time. (As we mentioned earlier, it is possible that once we become aware of the conflict, we may move immediately to solve the conflict issue without even talking to them in the first place.)

So if we cannot get my problem solved with them and it is critical that we get the problem solved, then we seek ways to solve the problem without them. We no longer view them as a partner but as an impediment, a road block, a hindrance or competitor. So now our problem becomes not finding a solution for the conflict issue, *but removing this person so we can solve the issue without having to address their concerns.* Being linked to them becomes unacceptable. We need to sever the ties of mutual dependency on this issue.

We search for unilateral actions that will address our concerns while thwarting theirs. This will have the effect of immediately speeding up the process of resolving the issue on our side as we no longer have to talk with them or worry about their concerns. While we will likely see this an advantage at the time, it is actually a disadvantage. Getting feedback on what will happen as a result of our actions is greatly diminished. This increases the chances we will miss something with our solution. We are digging in more deeply on our perspective. Additionally as we have reduced our communication with the other person, we are building and reinforcing the framework around them regarding their behaviors and tendencies that will create a false picture for us to recall going forward. And just as importantly, we are inadvertently assisting them in building and reinforcing their framework about our behaviors and tendencies. This significantly increases the chances of future escalations on other issues. We may have resolved this issue to our satisfaction but we may also have done permanent damage to the relationship.

In practice, this happens in two common ways. The first is going over the person head or behind their back or pick your own personal anatomic geographic metaphor. So if we report to the same boss, we go to our boss and tell her all of the reasons that we can't get our job done because of the obstructive behavior of our dance partner. We implore our boss to make the other person do what we want them to do. Best case scenario for me is, my boss makes this happen just the way I want. Mission accomplished.

Even in this case though, while I get the issue resolved, what has happened to the relationship? It is exceedingly hard for the other person to see this as anything other than back stabbing. Any future interactions between us will be marked by distrust and a lack of concern for the other person.

Something else to consider here is how likely is it that our boss will do this exactly as we desire? She will have to talk to the other person and, when she does, she will no doubt get a different perspective on the conflict issue than the one we presented to her. Then, what? Who knows? Maybe she will side with the other party. Maybe she will decide to do something that benefits herself and not either of us. Maybe she will decide not to get involve, "The two of you need to work this out."

Or, if we report to a different boss, then we ask our boss to talk to their boss and make them do what we want them to do. The difficulties increase when we ask our boss to tell another boss to make their employee do what we want them to. This is so fraught with organizational power and peril that few of us who have worked more than three days would expect this to turn out the way we wanted. Yet, we have listened to numerous stories about people attempting to do this. None that turned out the way the party escalating expected.

But you might ask, what if we *must* get this done and we cannot get the person to cooperate? Then, our suggestion would be to go the boss together as conflict partners. Each of us can explain our perspectives, concerns and possible solutions and let our boss settle the issue. If you report to different bosses, then a four way seems advisable. *In any case, do not act without them.* Do not abandon your dance partner.

The other common way that people in organizations act without the other person is to simply do what they want despite what the other person says or wants done. We just make it a fait accompli. Then the other person has to try to do something about it. Maybe there will be nothing they can do about it. We find a way of 'doing it' without them. We work around them.

This is actually quite common in conflicts between bosses and subordinates. People in positions of authority find it hard to resist imposing their way in conflicts with their subordinates. Why? Because they can get their concerns addressed simply by making it so. We have had those people in positions of authority ask why they should not get their way in conflicts, after all the organization has given them the power to make those decisions.

We point out two reasons. First, what is the effect on the relationship when we get our concerns addressed at the expense of our subordinates? Maybe we absolutely, positively, no if's and's or but's about it, have to have this done just the way we want it. (Be wary of making this claim, it is loaded with perspective traps.) Well then, if we must we must. We still have to attend to the relationship consequences. But, maybe we don't have that absolute, unequivocal mandate, then working the conflict through on some collaborative model would be preferable.

The second reason we may not want to do this is we could be wrong. Are we sure we see this more completely, accurately than they do? We're sure our perspective isn't missing anything that theirs can augment? We have seen just how insular our perspective can be. People in positions of authority need to more aware of this than others *precisely because* they have the decision making authority. It is not like everyone in every organization on the face of the earth can't give you chapter and verse on short sighted and mistaken decisions made by those above them. Here again working it through collaboratively makes better sense.

The distinguishing mark of conflict at Stage 4 (Images and Coalitions) is the conflict issue has almost disappeared from our attention. What we are focused on now is 'winning' the conflict by defeating the other person. Defending our reputation and damaging theirs are major concerns. In this stage, we have a fully developed disparaging framework by which to judge all of the actions (and inactions) of the other party.

As Jordan puts it, "These images are stereotypical, highly fixed and are very resistant to change through new information." Additionally, we will likely have attributed these same characteristics to others defending this person or belonging to their 'same group' simply by the fact that they belong to the same group. Interdepartmental feuds are notorious in this regard. These negative images of the other person(s) constitute biases about behaviors, motives, intentions and personal and group attributes. They form the framework through which we perceive and evaluate them. This framework creates an over simple perspective that prevents us from perceiving the complexity and nuances of the other parties behavior. We have a very difficult time seeing and naming anything positive about the other person. We cast our behaviors as simply reactions to the other party's behavior. In essence then, we are no longer responsible for what we do because "we have no choice". Their actions "made me" respond the way we did including any further escalations. Jordan points out that there are still some organizational rules that inhibition some kinds of my interactions with the other party. The escalating party adheres to these rules formally, but they take advantage of any opportunity to get away with unfriendly acts. Typical of this kind of behavior is some form of 'deniable punishment behavior.' The counterpart is incited, slighted and disparaged, but in ways that do not formally cross the etiquette line. Jabs can be landed through "insinuations, ambiguous comments, irony and body language". If challenged, the perpetrator can simply deny that any harm was meant. Often they then claim that they are the aggrieved party because of these false and unjust accusations. Knowing this since the other party cannot respond by openly discussing the incident, they may initiate some passive aggressive retaliatory action of their own. If you have ever been a party to this, you know just how poisonous it is.

We would also expect in this stage of escalation the active politicization of the conflict by trying to attract adherents to each side of the conflict. Actions ensuing from this are directed at gaining the upper hand in any power struggle through attacks on the identity, attitude, behavior, positions and relationships of the other side.

How far escalation proceeds depends on a number of factors, nonetheless conflict escalation is the likely consequence of the distributive path, of telling people about our concerns. This is the normal path. This is the natural path. This is the DNA path. This is the organic path. This is the intuitive path. This is the wrong path.

How can our intuitions be so wrong? Let's say we take a trip to Great Britain and you plan on driving there. If we follow our instincts driving there, what happens to us? We have a lot of accidents if we just to go on our instincts. We'll get hurt. We cannot go with our instincts. We have to think about what we are doing. And it applies to not just driving but walking around as well. In some places in London, they've painted the sidewalks at crosswalks saying "look to the right". Visitors step off the sidewalk instinctively look left to see on-coming cars. The problem is the cars are coming from the right. We actually saw somebody in London be hit by a cab who did this. He got clipped because cars were coming this way and he was looking that way. He relied on his instincts and his instincts sent him to the hospital.

As Kahneman points out about the instinctual response of our System 1 thinking, it is necessary and effective in situations that are patterned in regular and predicable ways. We do not need to "think about" those kind of things. We just do them without having to slow down to think (System 2). Instinctual responses, System 1, thinking fast fails predicable or when the situations we face are not patterned.

I think escalation is in part what gives conflict a bad name. This is why the conflict avoiders don't want to engage when someone negatively affects what they care about. Who wants to get involved in this kind of drama of negativity that is likely to damage the relationship or simply cause such turmoil? It's enough to send you home at night and start drinking for the wrong reasons. Ughhhh.

If we can't trust our instincts, we have to find another way. After Exercise 6, we will explore that alternative.

Exercise 6: Escalation stages in your conflict story

Using Glasl's stages analyze your conflict story.

What stages of conflict where present in your conflict?

Identify the stages and be very specific about matching the stages and behaviors were present for both parties.

What was the effect of the escalation on the issue and the relationship in your story?

Search for the integrative space

Recall that our actions to maximize the gains for us in the conflict situation marks the distributive path. We perceive that conflict as a zero-sum situation where each party tries to get a solution that gives them the maximum gain possible in the conflict process. It begins with us making statements about our concerns and needs and advocating for our proposed solutions.

The integrative path differs significantly from the distributive path. Here we are seeking solutions that integrate our concerns and our dance partner's concerns into a single solution. We do not read conflicts as zero-sum per se. We do not see the outcomes as either/or. We are looking for a superior solution, a more optimal solution for both parties. The integrative solution may or may not be there. We won't know until we try to find it. That is why we call this the "search for the integrative space." If the integrative solution is not there, we will have to find a just and fair distribution through compromise. Fortunately, the integrative space is there far more often than we imagine.

Imagine is the operative verb here. In the search for the integrative solution, we first have to imagine what it is like to be the other person in the conflict. We must see the conflict issue as they see it. We must develop empathy for their perspective. Sometimes people are afraid that if they are empathetic that means they have to "give in" to the other person. Not so. Giving in is not an integrative solution. While we empathize with their concerns, this does not mean we necessarily agree with their approach to getting their concerns addressed. After all their approach is negatively affecting what we care about. Once we have a more thorough understanding of both of our and their perspectives and concerns, then we are in a much better position to imagine possible solutions that might incorporate both of our concerns.

To begin the integrative approach, we do not *tell* the other person about our concerns. Instead we ask them questions that clarify the issue from their perspective. We follow up with deeper probes to gain more insight into their perspective. We withhold making judgments. We try to convince them to appreciate that we are making an honest inquiry. How will they 'read' this? It is unlikely that they will perceive this as a threat to what they care about. We are, after all, asking them to tell us about what they are concerned about and why it matters to them. Hence, it does not typically trigger the escalation cycle that we saw in the distributive approach. Explaining their concerns without being criticized or debated helps them to relax, become more cooperative and share information with us that often allows us to see potential for mutually beneficial solutions.

In seeking mutually beneficial solutions, we are not looking for a compromise solution here. Compromise is agreement through subtraction. We both have to give something up in order for us to get the other person to agree to a solution. It is the essence of the zero sum mind set: "What is the most I can wring out of the other party and still get them to agree? How can I get them to give up more than I do in the solution?" Let's examine the diagram below to see this in more detail.

Distributive Solution for 100 Units

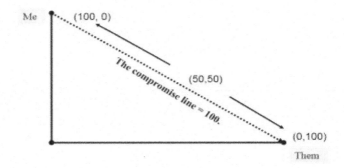

In this illustration, we need to agree on how we will distribute 100 units. It can be units of anything (ex. Money, respect, credit, recognition, status, etc.) Whatever it is, we are dividing up 100 units of it. We would like to have 100, in which case they get 0. They, on the other hand, would like 100 leaving us with 0. Now the compromise line runs between those two possible solutions. Every point on the line equals 100 units. Of course, many people think of 50-50 as *The Compromise* but that's not the only way to compromise where we get 50 and they get 50. We could get

75 and they get 25. That would also be a compromise. Or we get 38 and they get 62. Any and all distributions of the 100 units is a compromise.

In trying to increase our share of the distribution of the 100 units, we will do everything we can to get them to agree to move the solution to the upper left of the compromise line. These tactics might include arguing, agreeing, sympathizing, humoring, cajoling, guilting, threatening, tricking, debating, and lying . . . whatever we can do moving the distribution settlement in our favor. At the same time, they are doing what they can to move the settlement distribution down to the lower right. And so we can see that this is antagonistic and competitive and pulling in the opposite directions. Eventually, somewhere along the line, we may figure out an agreement but notice that if we going to distribute just the 100 units, it's a compromise. Both of us have to give something up what we wanted. Hence, compromise is agreement through subtraction.

This makes compromise the opposite of integration. Integration is agreement through addition. We are integrating or adding our concerns and their concerns together to gain agreement. To search for the integrated space is to get off of the compromise line, to get past the limit of 100. We are looking for solutions that are greater than 100. "How can we create a solution where we can get what we want and they can get what they want?" becomes our guiding question in the search for the integrative space. This is possible more often than most of us imagine. Too often we settle for a smaller share via distribution than we could have achieved in the integrative space.

The reason for this that, as we saw earlier, we approach the threat to our concerns by telling our conflict partner about our perspective of the conflict issue thus triggering the escalation cycle. Instead we need to ask about the issue from their perspective. This requires us to engage our dance partner in *a dialogue*. What does a dialogue look like?

Compromise is agreement through subtraction.

Integration is agreement through addition.

How is it different than a debate, or argument, or even discussion? David Bohm will be our guide here. In his book, *On Dialogue*, Bohm informs us that 'dialogue' comes from the Greek word *dialogos* 'meaning of the word'. *Dia* means 'through'. Hence a dialogue can be a conversation among any number of people. He says think of a dialogue as a *"stream of meaning* flowing among and through us and between us". This flow of meaning creates a possibility some new understanding will emerge that was not obvious to us prior to our dialogue. The conversation creates something new, which may not have been present when we began to share the flow of meaning with each other. "And this *shared meaning* is the 'glue' or 'cement' that holds people and societies together."

The dialogue is a conversation that opens up an interactive "stream of meaning" flowing through us and between us. This produces the conditions for us to generate something that we could not have imagined before the dialogue. Bohm points out this is not the same as discussion.

The word 'discussion' has the same root as 'percussion' and 'concussion'. It suggest we need to break things up to analyze then into their various pieces. Discussion is a type of verbal Ping-Pong, where people bat ideas back and forth. And like regular Ping-Pong, the object of the exercise is to win or to get points for oneself. "Possibly you will take up somebody else's ideas to back up your own - you may agree with some and disagree with others - but the basic point is to win the game".

In a dialogue, by contrast, nobody is trying to win. The point is to simply create a win. Dialogue requires a different mindset. We are not trying to score points, or convince others that our particular view should prevail. "It's a situation called win-win, in which we are not playing a game against each other but *with* each other. In a dialogue, everybody wins."

The distributive path and compromising are marked by discussion. The point of the discussion is to convince the other person to accept your perspective – to win the debate about who is right and who is wrong, who should have more and who should have less, what we should do and should not do.

The integrative path is marked by dialogue. We would put it even stronger. The search for the integrative space is achievable only through dialogue. As Bohm writes it is marked by "a different sort of spirit". In our classes and workshops when we ask learners what do they hope to get out of the class, the most frequent responses are "to add to my tool kit", "to get some new tools" or similar variations. It is also clear that those people expect these tools to make them better at convincing, persuading their conflict partners to come around to their perspective.

But the search of the integrative space requires more than just a different set of "tools". Although, we will need to develop a better set of dialogical skills. More importantly, it requires a completely different mindset. A mindset marked by being open minded - a willingness to examine one's own assumptions and perspectives, a willingness to ask rather than tell, a willingness to listen rather than a desire to be heard, and a willingness to say hard things without blaming anyone. Easy on the person. Hard on the issue.

William Isaac in his book *Dialogue* calls it "a conversation with a center but no sides". We are going to map Isaac's dialogue on to the conflict episode to show the connection between dialogue and the integrative path. With Isaac, it begins with a *Conversation*. Think of this in the conflict episode as the *trigger point* where we become aware that my concerns are being threatened. In the conflict episode's *intention phase*, we have to consider what we are going to do about this threat to what we care about. Isaac identifies this as the *Deliberation* point where we weigh out what we are going to do. He calls it a 'fundamental decision point". Moving along this decision line the first step is *Suspend*, which is listening without resistance. This matches up closely with our first step in the search for the integrative space, ask questions about the other person's concerns and listen without judging. From the initial questions, we probe for deeper understandings. Once we have done that, we are in a position to create a Neutral Statement of the Conflict leading us to identify the types of conflicts. This has marked similarities to Isaac's next step, *Reflective Dialogue* in which the parties explores underlying causes, rules, assumptions to get to deeper questions and framing of problems. Isaac's final step is *Generative Dialogue* where the parties invent unprecedented possibilities and new insights. This is our equivalent of what happens in the Conflict Solution Paths. Bohm and Isaac's work about Dialogue deepens our understanding of the search for the integrative space. Using their work improves our search successes.

Isaac writes

. . . dialogue is a conversation in which people think together in a relationship. Thinking together implies that you no longer take your position as final. You relax your grip on certainty and listen to the possibilities that result simply from being in a relationship with others – possibilities that might otherwise have occurred.

Conflict creates both challenge and opportunity for us to think, talk and act together. We are challenged to resist the natural tendency to respond defensively to the threat to what we care about. The opportunity arises from potential to find solutions "that might not otherwise have occurred." This is only possible, however, if we transcend our intuitive responses to conflict. Clearly the search for integrative space within conflicts requires a dialogical process of asking questions, deep listening, empathy and collaborative action. Only then can we hope to achieve the potential synergies generated by the conflict relationship.

Let's look in a little more detail about the process of asking questions, deep listening, empathy and collaborative action. Most of us think we are better listeners than we are. The famous Indian philosopher Krishnamurti in his work *Talks and Dialogue* cautions us

If we try to listen we find it extraordinarily difficult, because we are always projecting our opinions and ideas, our prejudices, our background, our inclinations, our impulses; when they dominate, we hardly listen at all to what is being said. In that state there is no value at all. One listens and therefore learns, only in a state of attention, a state of silence, in which this whole background is in abeyance, is quiet . . .

In conflict situations, we have seen this would be even more challenging. All of the distractions to listening that Krishnamurti mentions are heighten by anger, fear or other strong emotions.

In the search for the integrative space, we respond to the threat to our concerns by asking questions about the concerns of the other person. This means that we have to find a way to hold "in abeyance" all of our own personal perspectival noise in order to listen well enough to ask a question to open the dialogue. Not an easy skill to learn, not a habit quickly developed.

One suggestion is to practice this skill when you are not under the pressure of a conflict situation. For example, we can practice listening attentively, quieting our internal noise during ordinary conversations. We can do this by keeping our focus entirely on what the other person is talking about, to stay "with them" and not turn it into being about us. Even in ordinary conversations, without practice and conscious intent, this rarely happens. When others are telling us about something, we generally find ourselves interjecting back to them much of the noise of what is going on in our heads.

- Rather than simply listening to their stories, we often feel compelled to offer commentary, opinions and judgment about what they just said.

- Rather than simply listening to their story and asking questions to learn more about it, we 'hijack' their story by telling our own story that more or less follows the same topic.

- Rather than staying 'with them' in their story, we interrupt their story by asking close-ended questions that give us information we want or take the story in directions we want it to go.

- Practicing means we become aware of these temptations, distractions in our listening to others.

We need to listen - with the intention of simply listening and learning what the other person is telling us. We can practice holding our perspective in abeyance, of suspending our reaction to what we are hearing. We are engaged in dozens of conversations every day so there is plenty of practice opportunity.

Another suggestion is not to respond immediately in conflict situations, rather try to find a way to gracefully remove ourselves: "I need to think about what you are saying." Then in a quiet place, reflect on what we have just heard that would negatively affect what we care about. Recognize, by calling to mind, how our assumptions, values and other perspectives are operating. What is the person saying or doing that negatively affects what we care about? How does it negatively affect us? What is it about this that is hard for us to accept? What are they trying to accomplish? What makes this so important to them? What might we learn from their perspective on this issue? After some time for reflection, we will be a better position to explore the issue from their perspective.

In the search for the integrative space, we open the dialogue by asking an open-ended question about their perspective on the conflict issue. As they talk, we are bound to have some reaction to what they are saying. Often, our reaction will include judgments about what we are hearing. Our task is not to ignore those judgments so much as set them aside or suspend our judgments and remain focused on what we are being told. Our task here is not to render a judgment, not to gather evidence for winning debate points, not to gather information that confirms what we already believe. Our task is to learn about the other person's perspective on the conflict issue. What is it like to experience the conflict issue as they do?

The questions we ask should be guided by, as Edgar Schein puts it, 'humble inquiry.' We enter the dialogue by opening ourselves in a show of vulnerability. When we ask the other person to tell us about their concerns, we are admitting "we don't know" about this from their perspective but are eager to learn. As the conversation moves forward, we should be forming a stronger sense of who this other person is and what matters to them. We should be suspicious of 'the same old, same old' judgments about the person. What are we hearing that is new or surprising? What are we learning that could increase the size of the integrative space, create more options to get both of our concerns met?

This dialogue will likely not be completed in one meeting. Most likely we will carry on and deepen this dialogue across several meetings. The dialogue process should change our perspective by enlarging it with the perspective of my conflict partner. Ultimately, we are moving to create a neutral statement that sets us up to collaborate on a mutually beneficial solution.

It should now be evident that we cannot engage in dialogue without changing ourselves. This self-work is a prerequisite if we hope to develop expertise in dialogue. Bohm and Isaac insist that dialogue requires some significant growth in our inner development. In an interview with Global Leadership Television, Joseph Jaworski, another expert practitioner of dialogue, points out that Bohm stressed that our inner development must be based on self-reflection, meditation and contemplative work. The hard work of personal development is a necessary prerequisite to the full dialogue process. Without this inner development, we will be reduced to using dialogue in a superficial way. Without this hard work of inner development, we will not be able to set suspend our ego-centric perspectives.

Without this, dialogue remains a mere tool/technique and fails to achieve its true potential. It looks suspiciously like a form of manipulation. If others perceive that our listening and questioning are merely sophisticated means of manipulating them or the situation for our benefit, then they will not see this is not be a legitimate search for the integrative space.

Exercise 7: The search for the integrative space

Develop three possible open ended questions that you might ask your dance partner following your awareness of the conflict.

Shape your questions to develop a deeper understanding of their perspective.

How might you demonstrate empathy and concern for their perspective?

What do you notice about your own perspective as you formulate these questions?

Neutral Statement of the Conflict

The neutral statement of the conflict refers to a statement (or question) that specifies the conflict issue in a clear way that both parties can agree with. It is not an agreement about the solution, only the conflict issue itself. Three examples:

"It looks like the question we have to answer is which of these approaches will cost us the least amount of money." (Factual)

"How can we get your changes made without interfering with my schedule?" (Interest)

"Under these circumstances, you think the best thing to do is give the student a passing grade. I think that undermines our standards."(Behavioral expectations)

We evolve the neutral statement from our dialogue in search of the integrative space coming out of the intention phase of the conflict episode. Through our questions, we try to find out our dance partner's concerns that are being threatened. Our focus is uncovering for both of us the essential elements of the conflict. We begin with our dance partner's concerns first so that we signal our interest in their concerns and so not to trigger the escalation cycle. We ask questions, withhold judgment and build an appreciation of the issue from our dance partner's perspective. We are working our way to making them a partner rather than an opponent.

It does not mean that we am going to agree with everything from their perspective. But we are trying to change the nature of the relationship, to demonstrate some empathy for their concerns that are being threatened. If we can change the adversarial nature of the situation so that they see this possibility of partnering to find a solution, we will both learn something that will increase our chances of finding an integrative solution.

Fisher and Ury give us the sound advice that we need to separate the person from the problem, but it is not explicitly clear how to do that. We began looking for an overt way to create that separation. Over time through numerous workshops and conversations, we evolved the neutral statement of the conflict issue as a technique of separating the people from the issue while at the same time gaining clarity on the issue. As best we can, we need to remove the person from the equation, so our focus should zero in on the issue. We strive to get our dance partner to do the same.

Secondly, as we place the emphasis on the issue, we do not want to blame the other party for what's going on because then we would bringing in the back door what we had kept from the front door. In that case, we would be conflating not separating the two. Blaming the other person is being hard on them when we are supposed to be hard on the issue, and easy on the person.

This is also an implicit recognition that our perspectives are playing a critical role here. We will be better served by making those clear and explicit rather than each of us trying to impose our perspectives on the other. We saw in the Distribution and Escalation sections that is generally not a productive approach.

We know we are always dealing with both the issue and relationship. So we formulated our general orientation as "How can we make progress on the issue and maintain or improve the relationship?" Making the issue clear and specific constitutes progress. If in the process, we could also get our dance partner to agree on the issue that would be a significant advance. We would then be in a better position to address the issue in an integrative way. By asking questions about their concerns and not making statements, by not rendering judgments or trying to persuade them to abandon their perspective in favor of ours, we should be able to improve the relationship. Demonstrating that we are interested in seeing the issue from their perspective shows respect and empathy.

There is another important and significant advantage that comes from creating a clear and specific neutral statement. We can use this as a diagnostic tool in determining the kind of conflict for which we need to try to find a solution. Once we agree on the specific issue, then we can diagnose whether it's factual conflict, an interest conflict or behavioral expectation conflict (or some combination of all three).

Most conflict management advice seems unaware of this point. The methods that we use to address factual conflicts differs from how we address interest conflicts and then again from how we manage behavioral expectation conflicts. *Most approaches to conflict management fail to make these distinctions.* But just as diagnosis of types of illness and injury is a critical step in medicine, so too is it here. Failure to diagnose lead to ineffective prescriptions and inappropriate interventions. These inevitably lead to frustration and escalation. We will see below just how we can follow specific methods in managing each of the three types of conflicts in the most efficient and effect manner possible. While this does not guarantee an integrative solution, it does greatly increases our chances of creating one.

So how do we actually go about creating a neutral statement? There are a number ways to approach these conflicts issues. How the parties frame issue alters the way that the conflicts are perceived and can be managed. Sometimes the issue is obvious and the creation of the neutral statement is simple and straightforward. Other times, the issue is less clear, may be complicated by secondary issues that need to be sorted out and are not at all obvious, at least at first. In such cases, we may have to work through a few variations before we find one that both parties can agree to.

One way to do frame it might look something like this:

"This issue between us is - should an exception be made in whether or not these forms need to be filled out. Your position is that we should make an exception. My position is that we should not make an exception."

This has a couple advantages. First, it does describe the issue in a clear way. It is question of behavioral expectations about what we should do about the filling out of forms. And hence, we know what solution path we will need to follow moving forward. Second, neither party is blamed or privileged in the statement.

But there is a disadvantage as well. As stated, it sets us up in a kind of oppositional relationship, i.e. "The issue *between* us . . ."

It would be better framed so that we were partners in answering a question about what to do rather than a contest. So we might try something like this instead, "The question we have to decide is under what circumstances should we allow exceptions to the policy of filling out the forms."

This puts both parties on the same side so to speak. We are partners, at least formally, trying to work together to answer a question that concerns us both. It also recognizes *the possibility* that there may be exceptional cases.

This is an improvement over the first formulation and gives us a clue as to a kind of rule of thumb we might apply. Whenever possible look for a way for both parties to be working together to answer a question or address an issue where they both have concerns.

Here is an example that came to light in a workshop with a large regional general contractor construction company. As the general contractor, the company must hire a number of sub-contractors to do the bulk of the construction work. Despite careful planning, professional architectural design, prescribed bidding processes, etc., there remains the likelihood that changes in what was planned, designed, bid and contracted for will have to be made when it comes time to construct the building. When this happens, the question inevitably arises as to who will pay for the changes. Theoretically, this should have been made clear in the contract. In practice, it is not always that clear, or even if it is, sub-contractors may be asking for exceptions or relief.

How might we go about creating a neutral statement in such instances? The most straight forward way is: "The question before us is, who should pay for these changes? Your position is that we as the general contractor should pay. Our position as the general contractor is that you should pay." In an extended conversation about this, we evolved what we think is a better approach. "What factors should we consider in deciding who should pay for the changes?" This approach opens up more space for creating an integrative solution. The other formula sets up a kind of either / or debate that seems to suggest a Behavioral Expectation solution path. This latter framing opens up possibilities for a better integrative understanding of facts, interest and expectations.

Neutral statements in factual cases are generally better expressed along the lines of

- "The question we have to answer is . . ."
- "The problem we have to solve . . ."
- "The information that we need to find is . . ."

Neutral statements in interest conflicts are generally better framed as "both/and" propositions.

- "In this situation, you must get access to the new information and I have to be assured the information will be protected."
- "How we can get the changes you need without limiting the income that I need?"
- "We need a solution that gets you an increase in the budget without decreasing mine."

Neutral statements in behavioral expectations conflicts might look something like these.

- "You thought it would be best to make the decision on your own. I believe I may have had information that could have helped you."
- "You believe that I should always ask you first before making a schedule change. I think there are instances where that makes things too slow."
- "You certainly met the customer demands but I think it unnecessarily cast our employees in a bad light."

The Neutral Statement is a powerful tool for clarifying the issues, for building better relationships and for helping us diagnose the kind of conflicts we are having thus pointing us toward the right solution path. With practice and patience, we can become more adept at crafting these kind of statements. This greatly increases our chances of finding mutually beneficial solutions.

Exercise 8: Neutral statements for your story

Think about your perspective on the issue. Think about the responses real or likely to the open ended questions you asked in the search for the integrative space.

Now try to develop three or four possible neutral statements about your conflict. Which ones make the parties seem more like partners in pursuit of common information or both/and interests or exploration of differing understandings of appropriate behavior?

Think about making that statement to your dance partner – what would their reaction be?

Conflict Solution Paths

It is important to identify the source of conflict as quickly as possible. Failure to do so increases frustration, which as we have seen, encourages escalation behaviors. If we do not identify the source of conflict properly, it's going to take us longer to manage the conflict because we may likely choose the wrong approach to managing the conflict. This makes it more difficult to find an acceptable resolution to the conflict. It's also likely that the longer it takes to resolve the issue, the more likely it is that the issue will escalate. We wander around for a while. Maybe we hit on the right approach. Maybe we won't. But in any case, the longer we go without making at least some progress on it, the more likely it is that the conflict is going to escalate as it as stretches out over time. As we have seen, the tendency is for the conflict partners to start blaming each other instead of addressing the issue. They lose focus on the issue to be resolved and they spend their time trying to either score points against the other person, prove them wrong or figure out a solution that leaves them out of it. None of those things is good way to go about resolving the conflict.

As we saw above, the neutral statement of the conflict properly constructed helps us diagnose what kind of conflict we have.

Factual Solution Path

Recall that we can think of factual conflicts as disagreements over facts of the case. Each of the parties is making a factual claim. The parties disagree as to whose factual claim is correct. Or we might understand them as disputes about what the right answer to "the question" is. Both parties have an opposing opinion about the right answer.

There are some specific actions we can take to manage and resolve factual conflicts; we're going to call this the *factual solution path*. The solution path for factual conflicts is different than the solution path for values conflicts and it's different still from the solution path for interest conflicts. So let's look at what is the solution path for factual conflicts. We are going to try to turn factual conflicts into a joint problem-solving exercise.

Steps in the solution path:

- Step One: Be clear and specific about what facts are in dispute.
- Step Two: Discuss what information is missing that would resolve the dispute.
- Step Three: Agree where the information might be found and how to find it.

— Step Four: Incorporate more Information/data, insights and reasoning for a more inclusive, accurate and objective view.

The first step in the process is that we must be very clear about what facts in the conflict are being disputed. What are actually we arguing over? What is it that we actually disagree about? As our students know, "Specificity is a virtue and ambiguity is a vice." when managing conflicts. The neutral statement will have taken us a long way toward this goal of factual dispute specificity but we may have some further work to do even from there. A few examples may help.

We say they were warned about this problem; our dance partner says they were not warned about this. More specifically we need to explore *who* we think warned them. Was I the one that warned them? If not me, then who? They might be thinking that we are claiming that I warned them when I am thinking it was someone else. More specifically, we need to explore *how* we are claiming they were warned. Are we claiming they were warned in a personal conversation? Email? Phone call? Did the warning come in a report? They might be thinking the warning came via in person conversations and we are referring to a report that they were supposed to have read. More specifically, we need to explore *when,* we are claiming that this warning occurred. Yesterday, last week, last month?

In these kind of cases where we are in a kind of he said, she said recollection conflict, the more specific we need to be about what context of the claim, in this example of being warned, the better the chances we can narrow down the precise nature of the disagreement. This as we will soon see makes it easier in Step Two to make progress.

Another example is our claim that they made a mistake on our commission check. What kind of mistake? The pay period covered by the check? The amount? The data used to calculate the check? The formula? The more specific we can make the claim the easier it will be to move ahead in resolving the dispute.

A third example – they don't think our solution will solve the problem or we claim that our way of solving it is *better* than theirs. When we use evaluative terms like "better", we aren't going to have very much success if we don't define what we mean by "better". Does better mean faster? Does it mean more accurate? Does it mean cheaper? Does it mean customers will be more satisfied with the results? Does it mean easier to implement? Does it mean more in line with our mission, vision? We are seeking clarification by breaking qualitative terms into their quantitative specifics to as great extent as possible.

These are important distinctions to make when we are in disputes about factual matters. Step One is about taking the time and care with your dance partner making sure that you know exact nature of the disagreement. Once we have made this clear, we can reformulate our neutral statement into this form, "The question we have to answer is . . .." Or perhaps, "The information we need is . . ." These statement pivot from conflict into joint problem solving. We are no longer arguing about who is right or wrong. Too often in factual conflicts, we are involved in struggle to prove we are right and to get the dance partner to admit they are wrong. This is almost always a fool's errand. None of us wants to admit we are wrong. Even less so when others are forcing the issue. By reformulating or reframing this into a question that needs both of us to an answer; we are no longer advocates, opponents, competitors. We are partners in search of a solution.

Notice by doing this, we are gaining clarity on the issue. Notice by doing this, we are showing the other person respect and concern for their perspective; we are improving the relationship.

Now that we know the question we are trying to answer, we are ready for Step Two. Here we ask, "What information are we missing that would answer our question?" We need to converse with each other what information, if we had it, would resolve the dispute. This may be immediately obvious. For example, suppose we are arguing about whether we can promote someone who was just promoted six months ago. You say no we are not allowed to do that. I counter by asserting that we are allowed. We see we are missing information on promotional policies.

In other situations, it may not be so clear what information we are missing. For example, suppose we are arguing about what the meaning of some marketing information that we have seen. We will both be making factual claims about its meaning but we may not be sure what information would settle our dispute. It make take us some time to work through that question. In any case, if we had the correct information, we would not be having this dispute.

Once we agree on the specifics of the missing information, then we can move on.

Step Three. We need to converse about where the information might be found and how to find it. This is where we have to be flexible. It depends on what information were missing and what question we are trying to answer. Should we examine what information we already have on hand? Should we look for data that we may have but are not immediately aware of? Should we look at what anecdotal information we have? Should we look at what people have observed? Is the information in some manual? Is the information in a procedure? Do we have a policy that would help us with this information? Is the information in someone's head in terms of a recollection? Is the information in terms of their head in terms of their expertise? Or their past experiences? Is the information in a scientific journal? Is the information in a law case? Is the information available from a supplier? Do we need to construct some kind of study or experiment to answer the question?

Just where is this information and how to find it needs to be at the heart of our conversation. We are trying to think together about where we might find this information. Notice now what's happening here. We are not arguing with each other. We're not trying to show who is right or wrong. We're working together to determine the best way of resolving this problem with the additional information. That's a key part of turning factual conflicts, factual disputes into joint problem-solving. If we try to dictate the answer then it's not a partnership. Your dance partner may have ideas that you've never thought of. We can see again the importance of combining perspectives.

Once we have this information, Step Four is to incorporate this information into a more comprehensive view. To see this issue perhaps in a fuller more comprehensive or nuanced way. Recall the Coke bottle example. Each of our perspectives on the factual question was correct but just as important it was partial and incomplete. By combining all of our insights, experiences and observations, we had a more complete understanding of the Coke bottle. This combining will likely require more conversation and perhaps even more questions that have to be answered in the same way. It may also uncover aspects of the conflict that are interest or expectation conflicts.

Does this always work? No, of course not, but it does work a lot. The important recognition is that it moves opposition into joint problem solving. It clarifies the issue and helps build the relationship even if we do not have an immediate answer. We also have to recognize that the more complicated the factual issue is the longer will be the process of finding the answers to our question. In some case, we might be able to solve factual conflicts in a matter of minutes. In other cases, it may be weeks or months or . . .?

Behavioral Expectation Solution Path

Let's recall the definition and a brief explanation for behavioral expectation conflicts. They arise from our belief that the other person *should* have behaved differently than they did. Or flipping it, our dance partner expected us to behave differently than we did. "Should" is the key word that signals that we have a behavioral expectation conflict. We use "should" when we when we wish to indicate that there is an obligation of some sort to act in a particular way. We diagramed the conflict like this:

A situation arises – call it S1. Our dance partner responds to that S1 by deciding to act in a particular way – call it D1.

S1 = D1

When we become that our dance partner has done this, it negatively affects what we care about. From my perspective, they *should have made* D2 not D1.

S1 = D2

Okay this is a situational decision that we disagree with. We are looking at the situation S1 and we opine, 'what the hell were they thinking?! Obviously they should have done D2. What's the matter with them? This is a big mistake."

It turns out that this gives us a key to creating a repeatable method for managing these kinds of conflicts. It signals that this is essentially driven by our different perspectives on how people should behave in certain situations. The Harvard Negotiation Project has a website connected with Fisher and Ury et al. There are videos out there about this both for personal interest conflicts, organization interest conflicts and international interest conflicts - hundreds of articles and dozens of books have been written about interest conflicts and interest based negotiation. We have included some of that material in this book.

Not so for behavioral expectation conflicts. Despite the fact of the most common kind of conflict are behavioral expectation conflicts, there's almost nothing out there as a detailed explicit method for managing these kinds of conflicts. So we had to try to work out our own a methodological approach for these kinds of conflicts. How can we proceed in these kind of conflicts that improves our understanding of the issue and at the same time maintains or improves the relationship? We need to open a dialogue guided by these six questions.

- o From their perspective, what was the context of their behavior?

- o From their perspective, what choices were available to them in that situation?

- o From their perspective, what factors made their choice the preferred action?

- o From my perspective, what do I think would have been a better choice of behavior?

- o From my perspective, what makes that behavior preferable?

- o Future orientation: what should we do in the future?

From their perspective, what was the context of their behavior?
Now, we might think, "Do I really understand the S1 situation from my dance partner's perspective?" The chances of our misunderstanding

what took place are reasonably high given the fact that we are looking at it from our perspective, from outside their situation. Maybe we didn't get what was really going on. We know that our perspective is always partial and colored by our experiences, perceptions and memories. What are the chances that we might not have seen the situation the way our dance partner does? And if we are not seeing it the same, then it is not really an S1 situation. So we need to check. Is our understanding of S1 the same as their understanding of S1? From their perspective what does the situation look like?

We want the reader to think about their own experiences in life. We are sure that you have been involved in a situation where you said to a friend, "I don't know what the hell Mary was thinking. That was a really bad decision."

Then, your friend replies, "Yeah maybe but did you know that this is what happened before that?

You reply, "No, I didn't realize that! Now I understand what they did. Given that situation, their decision makes sense. You know what? I would've done the same thing if I were them!"

If you had that experience (We are sure you have) it means that what you thought was an S1 situation was something else. So what they were facing, experiencing was not what you thought. In short, you were mistaken about the situation.

So the first step in the process is to check to make sure that our perception of the S1 situation is the same as their perception of the S1 situation. The best way to do that is to ask them to tell us about the situation from their perspective. As Edgar Schein has written in *Humble Inquiry*, this has to be in the spirit of genuine curiosity and humility. Our ability to listen deeply here is critical to the process. We are not as Otto Sharma warns simply "listening to download" information that confirms what we already know. We are trying to learn something new. We are asking them to tell us about something for which we may not have the answer. We have to be prepared at this point to probe with follow-up questions to get a fuller understanding of their perspective on the situation. Calls for dialogue. Most importantly, we have to hold open the possibility that we might be mistaken about the situation. Only then can we see if what we thought was an S1 situation was what our conflict partner experienced.

The specific questions to ask will depend on the circumstances and our prior relationship with our dance partner. We have to be careful that this inquiry is not perceived by them as an interrogation. We must show that we are genuinely interested in learning about the situation from their perspective. At a minimum, this calls for open ended questions, a patient approach, withholding comments and judgments and some expressions of empathy as appropriate.

There are two possibilities that might emerge as a result of my inquiry. The first is that we gain a new understanding of the situation from their perspective. This understanding alters the way we view the situation so that we now agree with the decision they made. We have the "If-I-were-them-I-would-have-done-the-same-thing" experience. If this happens, then the conflict has been resolved.

The second possibility is that we have a better understanding of the situation and that it is consistent with what we thought it was. Or that it was different but not so different that it alters our judgment that they made a mistake in their response to the situation. In this case, since the issue has not been resolved, then we should move to the next step.

From their perspective, what choices were available to them in that situation?
Since we now know that we share roughly the same perceptions of the S1 situation, we can turn our attention to the D1 decision they made. We wonder why they thought D1 was the best response to the situation in which they found themselves. As with our inquiry regarding their perspective on the context of their behavior, we need to exercise caution and discretion so as not create a defensiveness in our conversation. We have to be careful that this inquiry is not perceived by them as an interrogation. We must show that we are genuinely interested in learning the purpose and reasoning about their choice. At a minimum, this calls for open ended questions, a patient approach, withholding comments and judgments and some expressions of empathy as appropriate. Did they consider other choices? Or was this a mere reaction? We know that in many situations our rationale for our choices is a post facto reaction construction. Was a D2 response even on their list of possibilities? They may not have considered it at all. An exploration of possible choices is should lead to an evaluation of those choices from their perspective.

From their perspective, what factors made their choice the preferred action?

Maybe D2 was available to them as a choice but for whatever reason, from their perspective, that a D1 response was superior to D2. Maybe it did not meet their interests. Maybe there was a rule against it. Maybe they didn't have whatever resources necessary to make D2 a reality. Maybe they had some moral objection to D2 behavior. They might not have chosen D2 for reasons of which we are unaware. It may turn out that once we understand the limitations on their choices, we will see that D1 made sense under those constraints. Now we agree with them because we understand their decision more completely than we did before. We think, "Yeah that was the best thing to do." We've had that experience in life already. This is not that unusual. If this turns out to be true, then the conflict is resolved.

It might turn out in reflecting on their choices they were unaware that D2 was a possible response to an S1 situation. If that is so, then we can ask them something like, "You mentioned several choices but you didn't mention D2 as a possible response to the situation you faced. What kept D2 off your list of choices?" We can either do that here or make it part of the next step. In either case, we need to bring it out as a possibility and have them examine it from their perspective. It may turn out that when we do and they consider it, then they will see that as a better choice. If this turns out to be true then, then the conflict is resolved because now they agree with us.

While I list this as a step after the exploration of potential choices, it is possible that as they talk about each potential choice, they will evaluation of that choice from their perspective. In either case, this is a critical part of the dialogical process for managing behavioral expectation conflicts.

Just as we saw in the case of the examining the differing perspectives on the situation, the dialogue here opens up the possibility that we are mistaken about the best course of action under the circumstances. The first three questions created the conditions where we could learn something new that would change our perspective on their behavior.

But let's say that even after this dialogue, we still believe that they made a bad decision. D2 still looks preferable to us. The next three questions are designed to get our dance partner to examine their decision to see if they were mistaken about the best course of action. So now our next three questions are the questions we pose in order for the other person to reflect on their choices based on our challenge to them.

From my perspective, what do I think would have been a better choice of behavior?
So we say to them something like this, "I've listened carefully to your perspective on this. I understand what you did and I understand why you did it. I appreciate what you were trying to accomplish but I think there may have been a better choice. Here's what I think was a better choice." We should expect a bit of a push back here, but because we listened carefully to them about their perspective without interrupting or making judgments, their defensiveness will likely be less than if we had generated an argument initially. From here, it is natural enough to explain our reasons for this.

From my perspective, what makes that behavior preferable?

"And here's why I think it's a better choice."

From here we can explain what recommends D2 over D1. This should be done in a way that shows them the advantages of D2 for what matters to them if that's possible. What D2 can do for them that D1 fails to accomplish. If we have done a good job in listening and asking questions in exploring the issue from their perspective with the first three questions, then we should be able to link our choice to what is most important to them. We are asking them to consider the possibility that they were mistaken. We have to do this in a way where they can save face and where they can get more of their concerns addressed than they could with their original choice. If we are searching for the integrative space, we have to show them they could have made a better choice even from their perspective. Specifically, one that got them what they wanted but didn't negatively affect us. We can ask them to assess the two choices side by side, evaluating the strengths and weaknesses of each approach. It is possible at this point that our dance partner may see that D2 is a superior choice over D1 in terms of accomplishing what was important to them. If so, then the conflict is resolved. If not, then we have one more chance to find the integrative space.

Future orientation: what should we do in the future?

If we cannot get agreement, then we would ask, "If S1 happens again in the future, what should we do?" Hopefully this allows us to consider the whole situation more widely. Maybe there are other choices, say D3 or D4 that we would discover in this wider approach to the issue. If so then we would have found the integrative solution. It is also quite possible that we will not find such a solution and will have to work for a compromise.

What recommends this approach to behavioral expectation conflicts? First of all, it clearly attempts to clarify the issue from both parties' perspective. Second, it treats the other party with respect, concern, and empathy. That will strengthen the relationship between the two parties.

The one of two alternatives in these kind of conflicts is to not say anything. Just let it go for fear of causing more problems or alienating the relationship. In this case, nothing will change. We will continue to be negatively affected by our dance partner's behavior. They will read this as their behavior is okay with us and continue to act in the same way. Over time, this creates a deep resentment on our part and what we hoped to avoid on their side – a rift in the relationship is now being created on our side by our failure to address this issue.

The second alternative is to confront the person with the fact that we disapprove of their behavior and they need to change. In the second case, their reaction to being lectured about their behavioral deficiencies is to dig in, save face, defend themselves and harden their resolve to keep acting the way they have been. There are many instances where the other party is willing to act differently if they are approached properly. If we tell instead of ask, then we will miss these. Instead this approach gives us the opportunity to resolve some of the hardest kind of conflicts to resolve.

Even if we go through all four steps in the method with no immediate change, we have clarified the issue and treated the other person in a way that builds relationships. This gives us the best possibility of leaving open the door to continued consideration of the issue by both parties in the future.

Interest Solution Path

Interest Conflicts arise from our perception or our dance partner's perception that we are seeking obstructive or incompatible interests. Obstructive or incompatible means that if we get what we want, then our conflict partner cannot get what they want. We view the situation as zero sum. The best we can hope for in this understanding is a compromise where we both have to give something up.

The interest solution path must begin with the rejection of the zero sum mind set. We have to be committed to searching for the integrative space. We will be seeking an agreement by combining our interests and our dance partner's interest into a single solution. So the first question we have to ask ourselves what are our 'interests'. To do this we have to be able to distinguish between interest and position.

Roger Fisher and William Ury have laid out the interest solution path in their ground breaking book, *Getting to Yes*. We will follow the general outline of that solution path and add some clarification and other ideas along the path. Here are the markers along the path:

> Separate the person from the problem
> Focus on interests not positions

Generate options for mutual gain
Insist on objective criteria

Separate the person from the problem

If you have been paying attention along the way, we have crafted all aspects of our approach to take advantage of their advice to separate the person from the problem. Suggestions and techniques for separating the person from the problem can be found in all of the other sections of the book so there is no need to do something with it here.

Focus on interests not positions

Fisher and Ury in *Getting To Yes* write that "Interests motivate people; they are the silent movers behind the hubbub of positions. Your position is something you decide upon. Your interests are what caused you to so decide." This is a good place to begin. We have found that generally people need a few different ways of making this distinction between interests and positions.

A second way to think about the difference closely linked to Fisher and Ury's is that interests are *what* we want and positions are *how* we think we can get it. This distinction between what and how is easy to illustrated with everyday common example that people quickly recognize and can transfer to other examples.

A third way to understand the difference that some of our learners employ is to think that interests are *our ends* and positions are *our means* to those ends. Ends and means is another common way that it is easy to find recognizable examples accessible for most people.

Some learners have found that thinking of interest as *a destination* and the position as *the journey or path* was helpful.

Whichever way you find useful, your ability to discern your interests and your dance partner's interests and to distinguish those from each of your positions is critical to the interest solution path.

Why is this critical for us? Why does this liberate us from the shackles of zero sum thinking? How does this free us up to find really creative solutions under the circumstances?

Fisher and Ury point out, ". . . for every interest there usually exist several possible positions that could satisfy it." Think of our destination and journey distinction. Suppose you want to go to Cape Canaveral to watch a rock launch. There are may be many different ways you could do that. You could fly to Orlando International and rent a car to drive to the Cape. You could fly to Sanford International and rent a car. You rent a car and drive the whole way. You could ask a friend to drive and share expenses. You could take a bus. You could take a train and then rent a car. You could use your own car and drive to the Cape. The conflict most often arises not over your interest (in this case going to the Cape) but your position, the way you decide to go there.

Let's extend this and see how such a conflict might happen. While you are interested in going to the Cape to see a rocket launch, your wife is interested in visiting her sister. You both have different but compatible interests i.e. watching a rocket launch and visiting a sister. The trouble arises if you both decide to use your only car at the same time. If you both dig in your heels about "getting the car", if you understand who gets the car as your interest, then it looks like you have incompatible interests. In that case, it becomes a contest of wills, a struggle over who will win and get the car and who will lose. It could get ugly.

Fisher and Ury point out there is a second reason this is an important distinction to keep in mind, "Reconciling interests rather than compromising between positions also works because behind opposed positions lie many more interests than conflicting ones." We can have compatible interests with our dance partners. As we saw in our example above, you and your spouse both have different but compatible interests i.e. watching a rocket launch and visiting a sister. We can have share interests with our dance partners as well. You and your spouse want a harmonious relationship. You both want the other to be happy. You both want the other to enjoy their free time, etc.

If we see compromise between our positions as the only way to solve the conflict then we will miss the possibility of both of us getting our shared or compatible interests met. This brings up a point we always make in our classes and workshops. We are taught from time we were toddlers until yesterday, that if we have a conflict we should look for a compromise. This is simply terrible advice although we often see it in some popular articles on conflict management. It originates from the zero sum mind set. To jolt our learners from notion, we have a saying,

"Compromise is for sissies."

Instead we should be searching for the integrative space. Creating or finding a solution that meets the interests of both parties is clearly a superior approach over trying to figure out what each party needs to give up to get the other party to agree. Both approaches require time and conversation. Why not opt for the approach that has us seeking ways that we can get what we want rather than ways to see how little we will lose?

Fisher and Ury give a good example of this with their story of the two children are arguing over who should have the orange. Of course since they have been taught that in conflict you compromise, they cut the orange in half. One of the kids ate their half of the orange pulp and threw away the peel. The other use the peel to make orange zest to make a cake and threw away the pulp. They both could have had *all of what they wanted* without compromising. The integrative space is there far more often than we imagine.

We have had numerous learners in class say that they had never even thought of an integrated approach since they always thought compromise was the only way to deal with conflict. The recognition that many people are locked into a zero-sum mindset offers us a powerful tool in dancing with our conflict partners. When we explain the search for the integrative space to our dance partner as an alternative to compromising you will be surprised how much better they dance. After all, we are going to help them get what they want, just not in a way that negatively affects our interests. In the end, if we cannot find the integrative space, we can work out a compromise. Since we have worked together to find an integrative solution, we both will likely have a greater appreciation for the other person's perspective and that should make coming to a compromise easier than if we started there.

In practice it is not so easy to look underneath positions to see interests. When the kids each said they wanted the orange how were we to know whether that was interest or position statement. Is this a "what they want statement" or a "how they intend to get what they want statement"? I have found that when you ask someone what they want in interest conflict situations, they will give you their position. The reason is almost no one thinks in terms of interest and position. (This despite the fact that *Getting to Yes*, The Bible, on interest based negotiation was published in 1981. Thirty-six years and millions of readers and folks still have trouble making the distinction. It also shows the power of the zero-sum mind set.) So we should be prepared to follow-up with some additional inquiries to help uncover both party's interests.

Fisher and Ury suggest you "Ask 'Why'?" as one way to discern if what someone tells you is interest or position. The reason they give is likely to be their interest (or closer to it, you may need an additional question). So in the case of the orange, if one of the kids would have asked, "Why do you want the orange?" the other's answer would have revealed their compatibility of interests. The authors also suggest, you could ask "Why not?" Here the idea is to ask why find out why our dance partners are rejecting our solution. The answer should reveal their interest. Similarly, we suggest, "What will my solution not do for you?" Or "What will having X do for you that is important to you?" Depending on the situation, we can fashion a question that opens up the space for the other person to reveal more of their interests.

While Fisher and Ury suggest asking "Why?" or "Why not?", we think we have to be careful with those 'why' questions. They can be read as an interrogation. Instead, we suggest using what or how as safer inquiry choices. "What do you want the orange for?" "How will you use the orange?' "How will getting this information on the form help you in your job?' "What will an increase in the budget help you accomplish?"

We also need to recognize that we all have multiple interests - a constellation of interests. Multiple interests increase the size of integrative space. We have more options from which to fashion a mutually beneficial solution. Furthermore, these interests have a hierarchy of importance to us. Not all interests are created equal. Their importance can shift depending on the situation. If someone in our family gets sick, we may find that our interest in their well-being has increased and our interest in attending a play has decreased. Over time, with age, changes in job duties, evolving family situations – can all lead to changes in interests.

This is why it is important to explore with our dance partner as many relevant interests as we can. The more we and our dance partner can openly speak about interests the better it is for both of us. We want to let our dance partner know that we are keenly interested in a solution that get their needs met as well as our own. When we do this, we may have to get help them let go of the zero-sum mind set. As always, specificity is a virtue. The more specific we can be about each person's interest the easier it will be to find the integrative space. Once we do this, we can generate possible options to meet the needs of both parties.

Generate options for mutual gain

Here is an example brought to me by one of my former students that illustrates the search for the integrative space nicely. George is a former student of mine and at the time that this occurred, he was the business agent for major university. All of the property and buildings at the university fell under his responsibility, about $1 billion worth of property. George's responsibility was to oversee it, to keep it in working order, to do whatever he found needed to be done. He had wide latitude in the job. The university needed a piece of property to put up a new building. An older gentleman had a small house on the property already. So George had an independent appraiser do an evaluation of the value the property to get an objective price on what it was worth. One of George's co-workers went to the elderly gentleman and said, "Hey, we'd like to buy this from you. We have had it assessed. Here's what it's worth on the on the market. This is a fair price." The owner said, "No, no, thank you. I don't want to sell. Thanks. No." So co-worker left and went back to the office. The people in George's office thought - okay the guy knows it's for the university. He knows the university has got a lot of money so he just wants to jack up the price. They went up to back to him and offered him 125% of its assessed value. The property owner, "No I really don't want to sell. Thanks for the offer but no thank you."

He sent them on their way. So they came back and said okay I guess he's going to play hardball here so we'll have to offer twice what his house was worth. He turns them away again. They went back to the office and told George. George said, "The thought occurred to me, well this is his position, not his interest. I wonder what is going on here. I don't know what it is but I should go ask what's going on. George went out to the house, said to the guy, "Hi, I'm George. I'm from the university". The guy says, "No, no. I've already told your people three times. I don't want to sell." George said, "I'm not here to convince you to sell. I know you don't want to sell what I don't know is why don't you want to sell." George was trying to get past position to interest. The guy told him, "Look, I grew up poor and always thought if I had some property I could hand it down to my kids and grandkids. I could have property in the family and so I got this small piece of property, and I want to keep it for my family after I'm gone." George said, "That makes perfect sense. What if I can help you do that?" The guy replied, "How could you help me do that?" George said, "What if we leased it from you for 100 years. That way you can be sure that not only would your children not sell it, your grandchildren and even great grandchildren won't be able to sell it. It's going to be with your great-great-great-grandchildren. It will be in the family for four generations. At a minimum that would make sure that what you want to keep it in the family would be there for a long time." The guy said, "We can do this." George signed a lease with owner to lease the property for 100 years. They both got what they wanted. No one had to compromise.

Once we know his interest, we could have traded properties. There were other possibilities as well. That's not the point. The point of it is by asking "why", George found out what his interest was. What originally seemed like incompatible interests, George discovered was really incompatible positions. Once he recognized that, he was able to create an integrative solution. So we are challenged to uncover those hidden interests so that we can generate possible integrative solutions with our dance partners.

Once we know our interests, our task is find ways we can get those interests satisfied. We need choices. Choices create space for solutions. The more choices the better chances we can find the integrative space. Creating choices is a kind of brain storming activity. We have to be aware the creating and critiquing are incompatible activities. Judgment inhibits creativity. So generate your choices first and then go back and evaluate them against each party's constellation of interests. In essence we are trying to solve each other's problem, looking for mutual gain, both/and solutions. What interests do we share? What means do we have actualize those interests? What differing interests do we have? These differences are very often the key to integrative solutions. Think about George's interest in getting a location for his new building and the property owner's interest in keeping the property in the family. The very differences made the integrated solution possible.

Being nice and giving in on our interests is not searching for the integrative space. If we give in on our interests, we have slipped onto the distributive path; we have acquiesced to the zero-sum mind set. The key here is to be flexible on positions while we are hard on our interests.

Know what our real interests are and stick to them but then look for a variety of positions that will satisfy our mutual interests. We will be rewarded for our openness and creativity in finding ways of generating mutually beneficial solutions. We have created a little in-class exercise to help make this point.

So let's say instead of the orange, we got a $20 bill in front us. If we both claim it, is this a true zero-sum situation? Is this truly not positional but interest conflict? Is there a way that we could integrate our interests here? On the surface, it looks we cannot. If we think about it, the orange turned out to be two things not one. But a $20 bill is clearly just one thing. So maybe we just have to give in and split it into two 10's. We don't really want to do that. You know because that's a compromise and we don't want to look like sissies. But maybe we'll be forced to in this case. Sigh, maybe we'll just have to be sissies.

I don't know for sure so I think I'm going to check with my dance partner José on this. I'm going to ask Jose two questions. The answer those two questions will determine whether or not we can find the integrative space. Yeah, first question, José. Are you emotionally attached to this particular $20? No? Good, good. A different $20 would suit your interests just as well. Great, you'd be okay with that. Cool, we're halfway home. The reason I asked this is maybe your grandfather owned this $20 and you're emotionally attached to this particular $20. I'm just checking, just being thorough.

Okay' Jose, now the next question is does it have to be this moment.

What about if you got your $20 tomorrow? Would that be okay with you? Tomorrow would be fine, great. Thanks Jose. So now here's the deal, here is my proposed integrated solution. José what I wanted you to do is this. I want you to go home tonight and make a list of all the ways you and I working together can turn the $20 into $40. I'll go home tonight and I'll make a list that I think we can work together to turn $20 into $40. We will come back together tomorrow and will compare lists and see what is on both of our lists. Maybe I'll find something on your list that I never thought of. Conversely, you can check mine to see if there is something there you never thought of. When we get done will take the stuff that's on your list and my list together. If it is on both of our lists, I'll let you pick any of those items and that is what we will work on together.

We've agreed to work together to meet our interests not to compromise, not to divide. We've agreed to probably share some risk. We've agreed to find a solution that creates more than $20. We are not going to be bound by the $20 zero-sum line. We have to create a solution that's greater than $20. The point here is that we're creating value above the compromise line. My suspicion is that we will find a solution that generates more than $40. We could keep working together so then we're establishing an on-going partnership. Hey, you know we might generate $80 out of this or $100 or more. The compromise would have given us $10 each and no possibility of a long term prosperous partnership. We pass up an opportunity to help each other prosper and we take this compromise solution. But instead, we believe in the search for the integrative space. We believe working collaboratively in dialogue with our partner we'll create value beyond $20 each.

Insist on objective criteria

Fisher and Ury include this as part of their process because it covers how to arrive at *principled decisions for distributive solutions*. We have not been interested in arriving at fair compromises in this book. Not that it isn't important, however, we have kept our attention on integrative solutions. Nonetheless, they suggest the following for using objective criteria, rather than tricks, pressure and leverage we saw in the escalation section: Use fair standards that are independent from either party

- Market value
- Precedent
- Scientific judgments
- Professional standards
- Efficiency
- Costs
- Court decisions
- Equal treatment

Additionally, they suggest these processes for impartial decision processes

- Coin flips
- Cut and choose
- Veil of ignorance choices – not knowing your part
- Taking turns
- Drawing lots
- Letting a third party decide
- Choosing the last best offer

These are all useful suggestions for making objective and impartial distributions for zero sum situations. I have included them to give the reader some ideas about what to do in distributive situations even though my emphasis in this book is on integrative solutions. Readers interested in how to do this can do no better than go to *Getting to Yes.*

Exercise 9: Applying the right solution path to your story

Choose one of the types of conflicts present in your story – factual, interest or behavioral expectation. Apply the proper solution path to your conflict type. Follow the path steps laid on in this section.

What possible solutions emerged from this exercise that were different than the ones in your original story?

Which were the same or similar? To what degree was your own approach similar to the ones suggested here? What was the difference?

How might you use these solution paths in the future?

This and That

Here are some other topics, we need to address when thinking about conflicts and collaboration.

Bosses and Subordinates

The relationship between bosses and subordinates presents special challenges in conflict situations. Many learners in our workshops and classes have told conflict stories with their bosses as their dance partners. For subordinates, these are typically stories of frustration and anxiety. For bosses, they too have expressed frustration about their conflicts with their subordinates.

In formal terms, bosses can simply dictate their preferred 'solution' to almost any conflict between themselves and their subordinates. In practice, bosses find it hard to resist the temptation to impose their solutions simply because they can. The pressures, especially the time pressures, bosses operate under make this seem expedient. Additionally, as we have seen, the search for the integrative space requires us to ask questions and practice, in the words of Edgar Schein, 'humble inquiry'.

Schein points out that generally corporate culture expects people in position of authority to tell rather than ask. In fact, for many in positions of authority, the idea of asking and humble inquiry often fails to even surface as a viable option.

This means that as a subordinate who has a conflict with the boss we have to be aware that we are working uphill so to speak. We have be especially alert for the boss's concerns and what they hope to accomplish with their solution. What are the benefits of their solution from their perspective needs even more scrutiny from us than when we are dealing with peers or others.

One of the things that we subordinates often fail to recognize in our conflicts with our bosses is the importance of precedent in the boss's preferred solution. We have to be prepared to address the precedent question openly. We need to fully appreciation that while the boss may have no specific objection to addressing our concerns the way we would prefer, they are constantly alert to either violations of existing precedents or creating new ones that commit them to courses of action they may not want to face in the future. Helping them re-frame the precedents issue can mean the difference between success and failure in getting your concerns addressed in an integrative solution.

We also have to be alert to the pressure our bosses may be getting from those above them on the food chain. Often they are responding to commands, demands and remands of which we are unaware. An integrative solution must include ways that helped them solve those boss's boss problems.

On the other hand, assuming we are the boss, we should make explicitly clear what the specifics of how our concerns are being threatened by our subordinate's actions or requests. But more importantly, at least at first, we should go the extra mile in questioning how their concerns are being affected by us. We should be extraordinarily slow about pulling rank merely because we can. We can and should remain hard on the issue but open and flexible on our position. We need to demonstrate that flexibility by resisting the cultural expectation of telling rather than asking. More time and attention to asking questions will improve both a solution and the relationship.

If we have to pull rank for whatever reason we decide to do that, then we have solved the issue but likely we have damaged the relationship. What to do about that? Make it the topic of a conversation with the subordinate. Our relationship becomes the matter of a new dialogue. Back to asking questions and humble inquiry.

Tough Cases

We made no bones about it. No one bats 1.000. The search for the integrative space will sometimes turn up empty. There will be no X to mark the spot. There simply is no integrative space. True zero-sum situation. Try as we might, twist, turn, re-frame – all to no avail – the integrative space ends up as the null space. If we have truly exhausted all efforts and methods, then we can accept this and try to work for what

Fisher and Ury call the principled compromise solution. Given that we have now fully explored the issue and done it in a way that tried to improve the relationship, then finding a principled compromise based on objective criteria should prove easier than had we approached the issue from a compromise mindset in the first place. So even in a failure of integration, we may find an improved measure of successful compromise.

Another reason we might fail is that sometimes our dance partners are just simply jerks and have no interest in collaborating even when they would benefit from it. Now maybe they are not jerks always and everywhere but they are with us on this issue at this time. Our assumption here is that you have, as in the failed search for the integrative space above, done what we have laid out in the book but it hasn't made much of a dent in our dance partner's willingness to address the issue. You can see the integrative space and likely so can they, but they won't agree to it. So . . . maybe it's you. Maybe your relationship is such that they just are not going to do this *with you just because it is you.*

In this case, you have a few choices.

One, you can just let it go. This means that you will not get your concerns addressed. How important are they? If not that important, then maybe letting go makes sense. Or maybe you can opt for a compromise solution where you give up what was the least important part of your concern.

Two, you could escalate the conflict. Move to stage three. Abandon them as a dance partner. Make the issue a fait accompli for your preferred solution without them. Go over their head. Of course, you have to be prepared for a potential ruined relationship and increased numbers and intensified conflicts in the future.

Three, maybe you are the wrong person to try to solve this issue. Does someone else you know have a better relationship with your dance partner? Would they be willing to take on the issue? You can share with them all the work you have done to uncover the integrative space. Best case, perhaps they can get a solution that you could not. Worst case, can't find someone else to do it, or they come up empty as well.

Four, similar to three, ask for a neutral third party mediator to address the conflict issue. This could be done formally through the organizational chain of command or informally with your dance partner. This has advantages over escalation by fait accompli or going over their heads. You are still engaged with your dance partner although there is an intermediary between you. So it is not a total abandonment of the relationship. Plus the mediator may be able to get your dance partner to agree where you could not. It might be a face saving move for them. They really did see the integrative solution but did not want it to come from you. Or perhaps the mediator cannot get an integrative solution but is able to hammer out a reasonable compromise. That is still preferable to Stage Three escalation.

Five, take on the relationship as a problem separate from the conflict issue. Prepare for a tough dialogue about the relationship itself. We will likely have to face some unpleasant perspectives and judgments about ourselves. We will also likely find out something about the other person that will surprise us. Facing them may provide a mutual breakthrough in the relationship that will make this and future conflicts easier to solve.

So even when you dance partner is acting like a jerk, you have choices.

Initiating conflict through organizational change

Most often when we think about conflict management, we are thinking about conflicts that our dance partner or we started inadvertently. Conflict management then becomes a process, as we have described above, of finding mutually beneficial solutions. In addition to these, we also recognize there are times when we need purposely initiate a conflict with our dance partner. The methods laid out in this book are expressly designed for these kind of one on one interpersonal conflicts within organizations.

When we move beyond these one on one conflicts, we recognize we may need to initiate conflict as part of organizational change. The search for the integrative space is not specifically designed to work in those contexts. We have already said no method works in all situations.

Still, we might ask, "What lessons can we draw from what we have learned about the search for the integrative space in one on one situations that can be applied here?"

As before we begin with a recognition of the importance of perspective. From our perspective, we see a need for change. From our perspective, we have a new vision for the organization. From our perspective, we desire to instantiate new values. From our perspective, we are headed in the wrong direction. "Our" can also mean those above us in positions of authority who have asked us to help lead the change.

Or it could be that certain changes are being pressed upon our organization by external forces and we must be the agents of those changes within our organization. Customers, suppliers, regulators, special interest groups, the environment, shareholders all may be pressing our organization for change from their own perspectives. These changes are bound to negatively affect what we and some of our colleagues care about.

In thinking about organizational change, we have chosen to follow Ron Heifetz and Marty Linsky because we think they are the most knowledgeable and thoughtful practitioners of leading organizational change.

Heifetz and Linsky have pointed out that these kind of organizational changes are often resisted because they mean that people are going to lose something they find valuable. Some product or process or position or way of life that is important to them will be no more. They are being asked to give up something they care about.

That asking or demanding creates a conflict. Heifetz and Linsky stress that leadership is about managing those kinds of losses. In our terms then, leadership is about managing conflict in organizational change. If this is about managing losses across the organization involving multiple people in a variety of organizational positions, then finding the integrative space is going to be extremely difficult, perhaps it could be argued, even a dysfunctional approach. Perhaps, but maybe the methods we have put forth still have some merit here.

In their book *Leadership on the Line*, Heifetz and Linsky begin with the recognition that the change needed is a particular kind of change. The change needed the authors call "adaptive change" – the environment that the organization lives in has changed. In order for the organization to thrive it must "adapt" to the new reality. Thus the environment, not the change agent, imposes the demand for changes. The authors go on to point out that these kind of adaptive changes *require people to change their habits, values, beliefs and behaviors.*

What exactly the adaptive change needs to be is unclear. What is known is that the old methods of doing and being will no longer work. The change agent does not have the answers to what will work. The change agent recognizes the need for change and engages the people around them to confront that need. The people that have undergo the change must themselves create a solution that is not yet know. The solution emerges from the engagement process driven by the change agent.

Notice in our terms, the change agent calls for a behavioral expectation conflict. Along the way though, they will deal with factual and interest conflicts as well. Those being asked to change their behaviors will likely dispute the factual claims of the change agent about the environmental forces pressing for adaptive responses. The things that they are being asked to give up creates interest conflicts. The role of change agent is to create all three kinds of conflicts. This makes the role of change agent so difficult and dangerous.

It will be instructive to compare our search for the integrative space with Heifetz and Linsky's approach to managing the conflicts they are creating. Our goal here is not to do a one on one, point for point comparison. Rather we are trying to find similarities in approaches as we try to understand how we can initiate conflict in a way that searches for the integrative space might guide us. The authors spell out their understanding of the process in five steps.

- Get on the Balcony
- Think politically
- Orchestrate the conflict
- Give the work back
- Hold steady

Get on the Balcony has the change agent leaving the dance floor and the action behind. The task here is about trying to gain a larger perspective on the whole situation. It requires the change agent to suspend their own perspective and observe what is going on from as many perspectives as possible – to try to achieve a higher level, more inclusive perspective. Over the course of the change process, the change agent moves back and forth from the dance floor to the balcony. Each time the agent suspends their own perspective and judgment and reassesses the range of perspectives of all of the parties involved. During these trips to the balcony, the agent is also monitoring the behavioral expectations conflicts and interest conflicts regarding people's reaction to potential losses. The ability of change agents to be successful depends heavily on their ability to understand the evolving perspectives as people try to adjust to the pressures of adapting.

Our approach also stresses the critical nature of understanding the other party's perspective and bringing that perspective into the solution space. Since the change agent is not imposing their view for the solution, they too are trying to find a way to meld these various perspectives together. This marks a significant connection between the adaptive change approach and the methodology of the search for the integrative space.

Think politically has the change agent developing a strategy of building a political movement inside of the organization for change. We have no direct equivalency in our method because it is aimed at individual conflicts not building a group movement. On the other hand, the authors imply that this movement will largely be built by working with people one on one in the process of creating an adaptive solution. In those instances where the agent is working one on one, trying to understand the other person's perspective and sharing their understanding of the forces of environmental pressures on the organization, then we would suggest that searching for the integrative space makes good practice. After all the more the change agent is able to create adaptive solutions that are mutually beneficial for more people the more likely it will be that these adaptive changes will be accepted.

The authors make clear, however, that as the exact nature of the adaptation becomes clear some people may have to be "left behind" because either they cannot accept the losses or their positions or divisions will be eliminated. In that case, there will be a permanent break in the relationship. No integrative space is possible. The search failed. Note that it failed only in those individual instances where no integrative space existed. In other instances, properly executed it may have revealed integrative solutions that are preferable to distributive compromises.

Orchestrate the conflict requires that the change agent modulate the intensity of the conflict. If the intensity is too high, then people burn out or give up or try to eject the change agent. If the intensity is too low, then momentum for change stalls and the forces of inertia doom the adaptation. The challenge that the change agent faces in this phase is to work out the differences in perspectives, differences, passions and harm to concerns in a way that minimizes their destructive potential while at the same time leveraging their emotional energy to create the adaptive solutions.

We would assert that trying to find integrative solutions is the optimal method to meet that challenge. Heifetz and Linsky recommend creating a 'holding environment' where people can safely discuss without fear of judgment or reprisals their perspective, ideas, concerns and fears. The integrative path seeks to create a space where people can freely and safely explore their various perspectives. Both require a space where people can reflect on the future course of action. The difference is that the search for the integrative space is seek to get the concerns of both parties addressed. In the case of the adaptive change we are looking for the optimal solution for organizational thriving. This may mean losing what we are most concerned about.

In *controlling the temperature,* the change agent increases the intensity of the conflict by continually drawing people's attention to the problem at hand

and challenging them to keep working on it. They are not trying to impose a solution. The best way to do this, we would maintain, is through the use of dialogue which is again consistent with the integrative path. Asking questions about peoples' understanding of the challenges ahead keeps the heat on the issue without making it personal. The agent can ask questions about proposed experiments and their results. These methods keep up the heat and are consistent with the search for the integrative space. If the heat is too high, one way for the agent to lower the intensity is by slowing the process of challenging the expected behaviors.

Give the work back recognizes that the solution rests in the hands of the people whose values, assumptions, beliefs and behaviors must change. It reminds us that the change agent is not "the solver"; they facilitate the change process. The authors suggest that the change agent make observations, ask questions, offer interpretations, take action. Making observations invites others to go to the balcony so they too can reexamine the situation and the multiple perspectives on the changes in process. Asking questions continues to open up the conversation about the environmental forces and adaptive possibilities. This signals also that the change agent does not have the answers but is seeking others' perspective. It keeps their focus on the issue and not the person of the change agent. The advice from the authors makes it clear that the questioning is true inquiry. After questioning, Heifetz and Linsky advocate an observation/interpretation technique. This clarifies your perspective on the issue and keeps attention on the work that has to be done. This can then be affirmed or challenged by others.

The way the authors talk about making observations and interpretations parallels the way we have constructed the neutral statement. We designed the neutral statement to make explicit what we thought the issues driving the conflict were about without assigning fault or privileging perspective. The neutral statement sets up the parties to take action to find a mutually beneficial solution.

The final suggestion from the authors, *Hold Steady*, counsels the change agent to persist in keeping everyone's attention focused on the critical issues needing adaptive work. They recognize by their comments that the issue may be evolving, ripening. They recommend again asking questions as the key method of understanding others' perspective on the evolving issue and problems associated with proposed adaptations.

Our purpose in this section was to see to what extent the search for the integrative space might be useful in stimulating organizational change. We outlined the key approach of the authors whom we consider are the most advanced practitioners of adaptive organizational change – Ron Heifetz and Marty Linsky. Clearly, change agents will find that the search for integrative space *is not a sufficient approach to adaptive organizational change*. Heifetz and Linsky's insights and approaches to facilitating adaptive change extend far beyond what we have laid out here. In instances where readers need to generate conflict for adaptive organizational change, they should take the lessons of *Leadership on the Line* to heart.

Having said that, we believe that the methods we laid out in the search for integrative change are consistent with adaptive change. Beyond that we think these methods can help change agents understand the impact of change from the perspectives of their multiple dance partners through the dialogical processes explained in this book. We belief that using these methods inside of the adaptive change process explained by Heifetz and Linsky can make the change process run more smoothly. So not surprisingly, we would suggest a both / and approach.

Preventing not avoiding conflict

We can apply the methods described in the search for the integrative space before the outbreak of a conflict. Knowing the importance of perspective, any time we are thinking about making a change in the way we do things, we should start thinking about how others may view this. We suggest going to those people who may be affected by the changes we are considering and asking them before we make the change how the change might affect them.

At this point we can begin the process of dialogue about their perspectives on the facts, interest and behavioral expectations associated with the proposed change before it becomes a reality. This allows us and our dance partner to front run the change and make adjustments mutually agreed upon ahead of the change.

This should significantly improve our understanding of the issue as we have engaged in an extended dialogue with our dance partner on their perspective on the issue. We know that our perspective is always at a minimum partial so getting this information ahead is a boon to gaining clarity on the issue. The fact that we consulted with them *before* making the change and that they can help guide the process is a sign of great respect and demonstrates our interest in their concern.

Objections to the change can follow the standard dialogical approach to develop a neutral statement and then utilize the appropriate solution paths to reach an integrative outcome. While no can promise that an integrative solutions is always possible this approach optimizes our chances of finding a mutually beneficial outcome. Even more so than in actual conflict cases because we have significantly reduced the negative thoughts and emotions that accompany a recognition of a harm to what our dance partner cares about. Our dance partner has an opportunity to participate beforehand in fashioning an approach that includes their perspective from the beginning.

We have also found that regular uses of this approach has the effect of improving the organizational culture by increasing collaboration and respect for diversity of perspectives. This generates situations for health conflicts to occur that stimulate creative conflict management attempts with lower levels of emotional stress and higher levels of intellectual engagement to find mutually beneficial solutions.

Today . . .

Sometimes no matter what we do, our search for the integrative space does not work out. Like trying to get that fourth hit in twelve at bats, many things, especially small things, impede translating our good intentions into a successful outcome. Too often, however, we see this as a permanent situation. In class, learners often say, "I tried to get them to listen to me but they are just too stubborn to consider a view point other than own. I give up. I tried and it didn't work."

The discouragement is understandable. The disappointment is keenly felt. We want to recognize the legitimacy of those emotions without encouraging people to give up.

We try to get people to recognize that this is only one opportunity to address the conflict. You will have other chances to try to get your dance partner to engage in the search for an integrative outcome. So we encourage people to end these statements of failure with the single word "today."

"I tried to get my boss to look at this from another perspective but he refused. Today."

"I tried to get my co-worker to talk openly about her concerns but she avoided the subject. Today."

"I ask my colleague many questions about what she want to happen next, but, she wouldn't respond. Today."

Adding "Today" opens us up to the possibility that something may change tomorrow that creates more space for finding an integrative solution. We want to be ready to persist to take up the conflict dialogue whenever we see an opportunity emerge that was not there before.

About the author

Randy Richards, Ph.D. is a second career academic, spent almost 20 years in management in both the public and the private sector before becoming a full time professor at St. Ambrose University. Currently he is Professor Emeritus at St. Ambrose.

He is currently a contributing faculty member at the Zagreb School of Economics and Management in Zagreb, Croatia; Visiting Professor at Kaiserslautern Technical University in Kaiserslautern, Germany, at the International School of Management in Vilnius, Lithuania and at the Berlin Potsdam School of Business in Berlin and Hamburg Germany.

He is an experienced facilitator and highly skilled workshop designer for adult learners and has an active consulting and coaching practice. Over the course of his forty plus year career, Randy estimates he has taught over 10,000 people across all of his courses and workshops.

He also has authored several peer-reviewed publications in general area of organizational behavior. He is the writer and producer of the video documentary, *The Heartland Highway Project*. He has also several plays including, *Sylvan Slough* which has been produced locally. His novel, a corporate thriller, *The Unseen Hand of Peter Gyges*, and his novel *Sid Hart in Cocoa Beach* are both currently available on Amazon as is this book, *Conflict and Collaboration, The Search for Integrative Space*. He has had poetry published in Quercus.

Graduated from St. Ambrose B.A. 1971, Georgetown M.A. 1975 and University of Iowa Ph.D. 1996, all in Philosophy

He and Dolores live in Rock Island, Illinois. They have four adult children and eleven grandchildren. Contact Randy at randyrichards49@gmail.com

Made in the USA
Middletown, DE
25 February 2020